Mushrooms

Wild & Tamed

Over 100 Tantalizing International Recipes

Mushrooms

Wild & Tamed

Over 100 Tantalizing International Recipes

Rita Rosenberg

FISHER
BOOKS™

Publishers:	Bill Fisher
	Howard Fisher
	Helen V. Fisher
Editor:	Helen V. Fisher
Cover Design:	Josh Young
Cover & Other Illustrations:	David Fischer
Inside Cover Illustration:	Bet Joy

Published by Fisher Books
4239 W. Ina Road, Suite #101
Tucson, AZ 85741
(602) 744-6110

Library of Congress Cataloging-in-Publication Data

Rosenberg, Rita, 1925—
   Mushrooms : over 100 tantalizing international recipes /
Rita Rosenberg.
     p.   cm.
   Includes index.
   ISBN 1-55561-071-4 : $12.95
   1. Cookery (Mushrooms) 2. Mushrooms, Edible. I. Title
TX804.R67   1995
641.6'58—dc20   94-37128
                                   CIP

Printed in USA
Printing 10 9 8 7 6 5 4 3 2

Acknowledgments

My deepest debt of gratitude goes to Bet Joy, who gave me encouragement and inspiration as this book evolved, soothing my frustrations and giving moral support. With her enduring patience, she spent uncounted hours on the computer deciphering my notes, writing and rewriting, and reinterpreting my syntax for the English-speaking reader. Along the way, we have tested and corrected recipes together, with friends and family as judge and jury. We have won every case, having indoctrinated a wide spectrum of ages to the joys of eating mushrooms!

Last, but not least, I thank Bet for the creativity and zest that brings this book alive.

About the Author

Rita Ruth Rosenberg was born and educated in Munich, Germany. She has traveled extensively throughout Europe and trained at the Cordon Bleu cooking school in Paris before moving to the United States in 1953. Since then she has received further culinary education in France, Switzerland, Austria, and Thailand.

Rita lives in Tucson, Arizona, where she teaches courses in international cuisine at Pima College, The Tasting Spoon and Culinary Concepts. Since 1984 she has been specialist for Mushroom Cookery at Fungophile, Inc., Telluride, Colorado.

Contents

Contents

Introduction

As a small girl, forays into the forests near Munich with my grandfather not only were delicious adventures, but also provided mushrooms and berries for our table. Later, camping in North America, I was appalled to hear forest rangers warning hikers of the dangers of picking and eating wild mushrooms, the gastronomic treasures of my youth. I wanted to cry out . . ."Learn about mushrooms! All but a few are wonderful to eat, you just must stay clear of the few!"

What a joy it is to see these old fungi friends increasingly appearing in markets, more varieties all the time.

My adventures in cooking began at my grandfather's side in the kitchens of his hotel in Austria and grand hotels in Germany, where he imparted vast culinary enlightenment to this rapt student. With this beginning, it is no wonder that cooking became the main focus of my interest. It took me forward to studies at the Cordon Bleu in Paris.

Years later, it took me to Siberia, where I was part of a group of 15 who traveled by helicopter to the hills of Kamchatka. Accompanied by a husky Siberian, a Siberian Husky and a dozen guides, we had come to hunt Borivicki, the Russian boletes. While stranded in camp by two days of rain we were visited by a regional shaman, who danced and chanted, calling upon the spirits for mushrooms and blueberries. Eventually both were found in abundance, and with hand-caught salmon, made up our every meal.

In 1978, after years of friends' encouragement to teach, I began giving culinary courses in my adopted home of Tucson. I continue to do this on a regular schedule, both at Pima Community College and in private cooking schools in the area.

The inspiration for writing this book came to me as I drove home to Tucson from Telluride, Colorado, where I had attended the

13th annual conference of Fungophile, Inc. This is a gathering of biologists, scientists, physicians and naturalists, as well as gastronomes like me. In looking to augment my personal collection of wild-mushroom recipes, searches through bookstores in my travels yielded mostly scientific and biological approaches to wild mushrooms with only a smattering of recipes. Hardly any books were devoted to the cook's bookshelf. So I set out to provide a volume for the creative cook who enjoys preparing novel, interesting dishes for family and friends, and who does the hunting and gathering at the supermarket.

Modern science is falling in step with ancient Oriental cultures, which have propounded the medicinal properties of mushrooms for centuries. They take them in teas and potions, as well as enjoy them as food.

As for me, I welcome with open arms the burgeoning appreciation of the marvelous world of mushrooms. I am eager to share my knowledge with a new wave of fungophiles.

A Poem

The Wild Mushroom

Well the sunset rays are shining
Me and Kai have got our tools
A basket and a trowel
And a book with all the rules
Don't ever eat Boletes
If the tube-mouths they are red
Stay away from the Amanitas
Or brother you are dead
Sometimes they're already rotten
Or the stalks are broken off
Where the deer have knocked them over
While turning up the duff
We set out in the forest
To seek the wild mushroom
In shapes diverse and colorful
Shining through the woodland gloom
If you look out under oak trees
Or around an old pine stump
You'll know a mushroom's coming
By the way the leaves are humped
They send out multiple fibers
Through the roots and sod
Some make you mighty sick they say
Or bring you close to God
So here's to the mushroom family
A far-flung friendly clan
For food, for fun, for poison
They are a help to man.

Mushrooms you are most likely to meet: Wild and Cultivated, Fresh and Dried

The Wild Ones

Black Trumpet

Black Trumpet, genus Craterellus, is also called the *horn of plenty.* In groups, these look like black tutus on stems, their scent is sweet and fruity.

Blewit

Blewit, genus Clitocybe, grows in rings, as in fairy tales. Typically has a blue-to-purple cap, gills and stem, and smells vaguely of mint.

King Bolete

King Bolete, genus Boletus: also known as *porcini, cèpe, steinpilz, herrenpilz.* Even a tablespoon or two gives a wealth of meaty, dense flavor to soups, meat dishes and sauces; hence it is an economical variety.

Chanterelle, genus Cantherellus: also called *eierschwamm* or *pfifferling;* distinguished by a slight scent of apricot. Light and peppery, it pairs well with cream. A black chanterelle is called *black trumpet* or *horn of plenty.*

Chanterelle

Chicken-of-the-Woods, genus Laetiporus: a large, showy mushroom with bright yellow-orange overlapping caps that grows in large clusters on logs, stumps or trunks of hardwood and conifers. Caps grow up to 12 inches across. Its flavor is strong and resiny, its texture firm and fleshy. Use this one in dishes that require long cooking times.

Chicken-of-the-Woods

Clavaria Delphus, family Clavariaceae: known as *coral fungi* and *crown coral.* They grow in little colonies of pinkish-brown and coral tones, often looking like tiny elves peeking up among grasses. Because they are sweet little fellows, they are also called *dessert mushrooms.* Delicious in fruit salads.

Clavaria Delphus

Huitlacoche, also spelled *Cuitlacoche:* genus Ustilago, a blue-black fungus that grows on corn ears in the field. This contribution to the culinary arts is from Mexico, where it is sought after by gourmet cooks. Called a *corn smut,* it contributes the essence of corn to crepes, risotto, enchiladas and in quesadillas.

Huitlacoche

Flammulina

Honey Mushroom

Hydnum Repandum

Lactarius Deliciosus

Flammulina, family Tricholomataceae: called *velvet foot* because of the dark and velvety appearance of its stem. Its color is yellow umber to orangy-brown with white-to-pale-yellow gills. It grows in clusters on hardwood. Surprisingly, its cultured sister is the enoki (page xvi). The flavor of the wild one is much more interesting. The enoki is mostly for show.

Honey Mushroom, genus Armillaria: wears a yellowish-brown cap on a thick white-and-rust stem. It clusters on live or dead trees. It can turn parasitic and decimate a forest in a hurry, so honey mushroom hunters become great friends of foresters. Honey mushrooms are wonderful in sauces and soups, and are great thickening agents.

Hydnum Repandum, family Hydnaceae: known as a *tooth fungus* because of hanging tooth-like spines that grow beneath its pale-orange, irregular-shaped cap. It also is called *spreading hedgehog, owl mushroom, lamb's foot* and *sweet tooth.* It is especially delicious in stewed-meat dishes.

Lactarius Deliciosus, family Russulaceae. It has a cup-like cap, orange with a fruity scent. Its texture is firm. These are a favorite of Russians, who eat them voraciously and as often as they can be found.

Matsutake, family Armillaria: jaunty white cap with brown scales in the center; its thick stem is as delicious as the cap. Its cinnamony flavor has a whiff of pine which comes from the evergreen forests of Japan, where it reigns as *the Japanese truffle,* not in taste and configuration, but in *value.* An American mushroom called *white matsutake* is similar to the Japanese variety, even to its spicy aroma. Interestingly, butter kills its flavor. Butter enhances the flavor of most mushrooms.

Matsutake

Morel: same as *morchel* or *morchella;* black or white, its smoky, deep, earthy flavor is wonderful with white wine and cream, as well as with roasted and grilled dishes. The edible morel is hollow from stem to crown, its many chambered and wrinkly exterior provides good hiding places for dirt. Morels take extra cleaning (see page xviii), but are well worth the time, second only to the truffle as a prize of mushroom lovers.

Morel

Pleurotus Ostreatus: oyster mushroom; cap white to brown. The complexity of its flavor and texture will enchant you. They grow in multitudes, overlapping one another, looking like tiers of choraliers wearing great white hats. Use them as substitutes for, or in conjunction with sea oysters. Enjoy them as a much more interesting choice in recipes calling for the common button variety.

Oyster Mushroom

Pleuteus Cervinus

Puffball

Russula

Shaggy Mane

Pleuteus Cervinus or Deer Mushroom, genus Pluteaceae: Fawn-colored convex caps sit upon sturdy straight stalks, their gills white to salmon pink. Its flavor is undistinguished, but it adds texture to a dish.

Puffball, genera Lycoperdon and Calvatia: At a gathering of Fungophile, Inc., a Colorado Mycological Society, an enormous puffball was found. Larger than a basketball, the puffball provided 20 pies for the wedding of Fungophile tour guide John Sir Jesse and his bride Ulli on opening day of the mushroom festival! Usually puffballs are small clusters of spheres in shades of white to tan, covered with little knobby formations.

Russula, family Russulaceae: Red to purple to olive-brown, this mushroom is often called the *shellfish russula* because of its taste and the texture it assumes when cooked. Indeed, it is a fine stand-in for fish and shrimp, but doesn't mix with other mushrooms. Raw, it is quite brittle and requires gentle handling.

Shaggy Mane, genus Coprinus: Sports a cylindrical cap with shaggy scales from white to reddish-brown. Its stalk has a movable ring! Shaggy Manes are fragile and soon after picking melt to inedible ink. For more longevity, hunters immerse them immediately in water and refrigerate them quickly. If you find them at the market, do the same.

Truffle: though dressed like a peasant and hiding underground, the truffle unmasked is the noble aristocrat of all edible fungi. The intrigue that occurs in truffled woods during the winter harvest is rife with secrets, skullduggery and chicanery, and always ending with prices most imperial. Gourmands worldwide overlook the cost and skip a meal to indulge their palates with this pungent darling. Tales abound from ancient civilizations of its aphrodisiacal properties. Indeed, its seekers and the dogs and pigs used to hunt truffles identify its presence by the scent of androsterone, the potent steroidal sexual attractant it contains. Author George Sand called it *the black magic apple of love.*

Truffle

The Cultivated Class

Picture the multitude of scientific sherlocks who, throughout the ages, have sought to expose the reproductive secrets of mushrooms' private lives, only to have them escape back to their wild, unpredictable ways. Only a few varieties have been coaxed into cultivation, among them these seven:

Agaricus: also known as *meadow mushroom, champignon* and *feldegerling.* Thick, woodsy and flavorful, it is hard to believe that this marvel is forefather of the common button mushroom. Parasols and Lepiota are also Agaricus mushrooms.

Agaricus

Crimini

Enoki

Oyster

Portobello

Shiitake

Crimini: a mild, unassertive mushroom that enhances the presence of other varieties in a dish.

Enoki: tiny pure white caps on slender stems are cultivated in tubes. Flavor is elusive, perhaps a breath of white grape. Primarily used for crunch and garnish, they are considered a source of healthful amino acids.

Oyster: use this beautiful, moist mushroom in place of the button mushrooms called for in cooked recipes you have been using. Oysters are easily cultivated, and as a result are becoming more and more popular worldwide. Like its wild sister, it is luscious in creamy dishes or brushed with butter and broiled until its ruffly edges are crisp.

Portobello: one of the big boys, a slab of which will grill like a piece of meat and, indeed, even substitute for meat. Chopped or sliced, it lends drama to a sauce or soup. It is quite imposing with its black gills and rich brown cap.

Shiitake: same as black forest, this dried black mushroom is found in Asian and Oriental markets, also fresh in most markets these days. Most widely cultivated of all mushrooms, shiitakes are a favorite of vegetarians as a satisfying substitute for meat.

Wood ear: has no stem, and grows straight to the tree, rather like an ear. Gelatinous when wet, it doesn't look too palatable, but don't shy away from this unusual specimen. What dash and drama it gives to a dish with its unique texture and shiny black color! If it's dried when you get it, best have a big container for its soaking. In water, these personify the word *mushroom*, doubling, even tripling their size.

Consider mushrooms as interchangeable: These are but a few of the mushroom varieties you are likely to see as grocers continue widening their focus on new products from around the world, and as cultivation techniques evolve. Just remember that any of these mushrooms may be used in any of these recipes.

There are a few recipes where I feel a substitution would make the dish less memorable. But do your own experimenting. Using this book as a guide, you will discover a world of cooking and eating enjoyment as you explore the mushroom kingdom.

By the way, I know that there are those who say they don't like mushrooms—based on the taste and texture of the market variety. It is safe to say that experiencing the taste and texture of the wild ones is another thing altogether.

Caution!
*Do not gather wild mushrooms without
an expert to guide you.*

How-to Notes
About Mushrooms

Selecting and Buying: Mushrooms should be moist and firm. Sniff them. If they smell woodsy, they are fresh.

Cleaning: Because mushrooms readily absorb water, clean them with a damp paper towel or a soft brush instead of washing them, which causes them to lose texture. Cut away any soft spots and clumps of sand.

Storing: Put fresh mushrooms in paper bags, not plastic, in the refrigerator. They will stay fresh up to 3 days, but it is best to cook them right away.

Preparing and Preserving: Slice and sauté fresh mushrooms over medium high heat in butter or oil (yes, you may use the lowfat kinds) for about 5 minutes, using 3 tablespoons oil or butter to 1 cup mushrooms. Cooked mushrooms will retain texture and flavor in the refrigerator for up to a week, in the freezer indefinitely. Never freeze fresh ones without cooking first.

Soaking Dried Mushrooms: Use water, white or red wine, milk, consommé, soup stock or whatever your recipe specifies. Soaking time will vary depending on factors such as the variety of mushroom and temperature of soaking liquid. Strain soaking liquid through a fine strainer or coffee filter. If you don't use the liquid in your recipe, freeze it in ice trays and transfer to a plastic freezer bag to use later for a quick infusion of mushroom flavor.

Fresh vs. Dried Mushrooms: As a general rule, 1 lb. of fresh mushrooms equals 1 oz. of dried. In a recipe, this is usually enough to serve 4 to 6 people.

Substitutions—Mushroom for Mushroom: you may substitute any wild or cultivated mushrooms for those suggested in these recipes. Experiment! Like fine cooks everywhere, use what is available and in season. But with so many dried varieties now readily available, you never have to yearn for mushrooms!

A Word to the Wise— Identifying Mushrooms

The best advice is to leave identification to the experts and your grocer. Hunting wild mushrooms is fun, but some will make you ill, and a few are deadly poisonous. If you are intent on the hunt, there are many books and teachers to guide and educate you.

Rita Talks Wild Mushrooms

On my palate, the succulent texture of wild mushrooms and the rich flavor they impart to food can find no peer in cultivated varieties. Yet absent the wild ones, I will let them into my kitchen . . . welcome them, even. To be fair, recent cultivation techniques and the quality and diversity of scientifically produced specimens are dimming the differences and easing my prejudice. Plus, convenience and availability do carry a bit of weight.

Still, I find no substitute for the sense of primal purity in the dank wilderness, and the joy of finding a beautiful mushroom, each specimen a masterpiece of form, color and even function. As an intrinsic lover of food and adventure, I was drawn even as a child to the mountains and forests of my native Munich, Germany, where mushroom hunts yielded baskets full of fungi for our table. Years later in the United States, imagine my joy at discovering Fungophile, Inc., an organization of serious mycological enthusiasts. This invigorating alliance has taken me to Indonesia, the Near, Middle and Far East, Madagascar, South America, Alaska, Africa, India, New Zealand and points in the Southeast Archipelago, including Burma and Borneo. My most recent trip was to Siberia.

In Paris at the Cordon Bleu, wild mushrooms are as basic to the chef as pepper and salt. In my studies I learned even more sophisticated ways to use the many varieties available to us.

The exploration continues through my teaching, as well as through my personal pursuit of new adventures in cooking. The following pages contain a collection of my favorite mushroom recipes, along with some miscellaneous recipes you might find useful. Along the way, you'll encounter a few tips, a little history and a few anecdotes from the hunt.

Recipes included serve 4 to 6 people unless otherwise indicated. So go buy some mushrooms and let's cook!

Bon Appetit . . . Guten Apetit . . . Enjoy!

Appetizers

Asian Abalone with Oyster Mushrooms

Pleurotus ostreatus, white oyster mushrooms, and abalone create distinctive texture and flavor.

2 cups chicken or vegetable broth

1 lb. large spinach or lettuce leaves

1 (14-3/4 oz.) can abalone

2 tablespoons oil

3 tablespoons oyster sauce*

1/2 teaspoon soy sauce

1/2 teaspoon sugar

1 lb. mushrooms

1 tablespoon cornstarch

1 tablespoon cold water

1 tablespoon sesame oil

In a medium saucepan, bring broth to a boil and blanch spinach or lettuce for 10 seconds. Remove with slotted spoon and drain. Slice abalone into rounds and blanch in stock 5 seconds. Remove and set aside. To a large skillet add 2 tablespoons oil and 1 cup of the broth and bring to a boil. Add oyster sauce, soy sauce, sugar, abalone slices and mushrooms. Combine cornstarch and water. Add to mixture in skillet and stir until thickened. Add sesame oil. On a platter arrange spinach and abalone slices with mushrooms on top. Serves 4.

Pleurotus ostreatus, the lovely white oyster, grows on dead hardwood in shelf-like groups: Fan-shaped and smooth, 2 to 8 inches in width, cream to slate-gray in color.

* Oyster sauce is found in the Asian food section of your market.

Chicken Liver Paté
with Wild Mushrooms

Wild mushrooms lend extra succulence to liver paté. Any liver may be used, from calves' liver to goose liver. Boletes or portobello are good choices for mushrooms.

1/2 lb. butter

1/2 lb. fresh wild mushrooms or 1/2 oz. dried soaked

5 to 6 green onions, white part only, minced

4 to 6 garlic cloves, chopped

2/3 cup Chardonnay or dry white wine

1 lb. chicken livers

1 teaspoon Italian herb seasoning

1 teaspoon dry mustard

Garlic toast or crackers

In a large skillet melt 1/4 lb. butter and sauté mushrooms with onions and garlic for 5 minutes. Add wine and livers, cook until livers are tender and liquid is reduced by half. Put into blender with remaining 1/4 lb. butter and seasonings. Blend until smooth or to desired consistency. Refrigerate 24 hours before serving. Spread on garlic toast or crackers. Makes 2 cups.

As Rita Tells It

A Burmese Adventure

The shiny brass shone on an old coach which had been left behind by the British upon exiting Burma. The coach was returning me from an early trip to a market some hours away from Mandalay. Because even early morning was hot and humid, and to have a better view, I chose to sit on top next to the driver.

The horse was going a speedy gait around a bend in the road which ran beside a deep, but well-vegetated ditch. Suddenly, I spied a succulent patch of mushrooms and gave a shriek of excitement.

I was excited, the driver was excited, and so was the horse. In any case, it all added up—the speed and the squeal, the excitement—and we all tumbled into the ditch. Relieved to discover our bodies were not injured, I abandoned the mushrooms. After some righting of vehicle and horse, we were on our way. Once I had collected myself, I enjoyed a meal of Burmese split-pea fritters called *Bey Akyaw*. Recipe follows.

Bey Akyaw

(Burmese Split-Pea Patties)

You do not need a Burmese adventure to appreciate this delicious appetizer.

6 cups cold water

1 cup dried split peas

2 green onions, chopped

1 large mushroom, chopped

2 fresh hot, small red chiles, chopped

1/2 teaspoon turmeric or chili powder

Salt to taste

6 tablespoons oil for frying

In 6 cups of water, soak the peas 6 hours. Drain and grind to paste in food processor or blender. Mix in onion, chopped mushroom, chiles, turmeric and salt to taste. Form 1/2-inch-thick patties. Heat 2 tablespoons oil in a large skillet and fry over medium heat about 5 minutes on each side until golden, adding more oil as needed. Makes 8 patties.

Chinese Stewed Pork Rolls

An unusual piquant and pretty appetizer.

Marinade, below

1 lb. boneless pork tenderloin

4 cups water

5 to 6 green onions

7 shiitake mushrooms, soaked, stems removed and discarded

1 (4 oz.) can water chestnuts, drained

2 cups oil

1 teaspoon sugar

3 tablespoons rice vinegar

1 teaspoon sesame oil

Marinade

5 tablespoons tamari sauce

1 tablespoon dry white wine

Mix tamari sauce and wine to make marinade. Soak meat in marinade about 30 minutes. Remove and dry with paper towels. Drain mushrooms and cut in half. In a medium saucepan, bring 1 cup water to a boil and blanch whole green onions for 2 minutes. Remove, drain and cut into lengthwise slices to use as ties. Cut pork into 14 slices and pound between layers of waxed paper until thin. On each slice place a half mushroom and a water chestnut and wrap into rolls, tying each with a green-onion strip. In a wok heat 2 cups oil to 350F (180C). Fry rolls 1 minute, remove and drain. Or, you may sauté them in a little oil in a skillet. In a 4-quart pan combine marinade, sugar, vinegar and 3 cups water. Bring to a boil. Drop in rolls and simmer 20 minutes. Remove rolls. Reduce liquid to half a cup over high heat. Add sesame oil and pour over rolls. Serves 4.

Grilled Matsutake

Matsutake is the gem of Japanese mushrooms, sometimes called the Japanese truffle. *For centuries, the Japanese have revered this elusive and rare mushroom for its delicious taste, as well as its medicinal properties. The North American Matsutake grows in the Northwest area of the United States.*

Dipping Sauce, below

2 large mushrooms

Dipping Sauce

5 tablespoons tamari sauce

3 tablespoons soy sauce

2 tablespoons water

1 tablespoon Mirin*

1 teaspoon sugar

1/2 teaspoon ginger, freshly grated

2 scallions, white part only, finely chopped

In a small bowl, combine all dipping-sauce ingredients. Light coals in hibachi or grill. When coals have turned white, oil the grill. Wipe mushrooms with a damp cloth, trim the stems to remove grit and slice the whole mushroom horizontally. Spray with olive-oil cooking spray. Place on grill and cook 1 to 2 minutes each side. Serve with dipping sauce. Serves 2.

Matsutake is from the genus Armillaria. Species is Ponderosa. It is a rare species found in parts of Japan from November to February.

* Mirin is a sweet rice wine found in Asian markets.

As Rita Tells It

A Tale from the Vienna Woods

Waltzing through the woods of Vienna with my friend John, sniffing the air for the scent of apricot that signals the presence of chanterelles, we came upon a mass of mushrooms that looked like a crowd caught in a sudden storm, yellow and orange umbrellas blown inside out!

Chanterelles!

Feast!

John insisted that the best possible way to prepare chanterelles is as follows:

Quickly sauté cleaned chanterelles in oil and as the juices seep out, mix in a little oatmeal. Sprinkle with parsley and lemon juice and devour.

John says you must use your own judgement as to the amount of oatmeal.

*Vegetarians consider mushrooms
the gustatory equivalent of
meat, in both texture and
ingratiating quality.*

Marinated Chanterelles

If you have marinated ordinary mushrooms, you will find new and delicious depth of taste with the wild ones.

1/4 cup olive oil

3 tablespoons white wine

1 tablespoon green onion, minced

1 garlic clove, minced

Salt and pepper to taste

1 cup fresh mushrooms (chop large ones, leave small ones whole)

Juice of half a lemon

Combine olive oil with wine, onion, garlic, salt and pepper. In a small bowl pour mixture over raw chanterelles; cover and refrigerate overnight. In a small skillet, place marinated mushrooms and their marinade and cook over medium heat 5 minutes, turning occasionally. Squeeze on a little lemon juice and serve.
Makes 1 cup.

Honey Mushrooms à la Greque

Honey mushrooms may be found in some specialty markets packaged in large, wide-mouth plastic containers. The suillus variety lends itself to this exceptional Greek appetizer.

1 cup vegetable or chicken stock, page 29

1/2 cup cider vinegar

1/2 cup olive oil

1 teaspoon pickling salt

2 sprigs parsley

10 peppercorns

10 juniper berries

1/2 teaspoon dried basil

1 green onion

10 fresh mushrooms or more, if small (about 2 cups)

In a 3-quart saucepan, bring stock to a boil with vinegar, olive oil, pickling salt, parsley, peppercorns, juniper berries, basil and green onion. Add the mushrooms and simmer 20 minutes. Remove mushrooms, place in a large jar. Strain the liquid, pressing liquid from the green onion, and pour over the mushrooms. Let stand at least 1 hour. For longer storage, cover and refrigerate until needed. Makes 2 cups.

Stuffed Mushroom Caps

Shiitake mushrooms and capers combine for a unique taste duo in this stylish appetizer.

16 large fresh shiitake mushrooms

1/4 cup fine dry breadcrumbs

1 tablespoon lemon juice

1/8 teaspoon garlic powder

1/8 teaspoon fresh rosemary

1/8 teaspoon fresh marjoram

1/4 cup finely chopped almonds

1 tablespoon capers, finely minced

2 tablespoons butter

1 tablespoon finely minced Italian parsley

Butter a shallow baking pan. Preheat oven to 350F (180C). Clean mushrooms, remove stems and discard. In a small bowl combine breadcrumbs, lemon juice, garlic powder, rosemary, marjoram, almonds and capers. Spoon mixture into mushroom caps and place in the prepared pan. Dot each with butter and bake for 20 minutes. Serve sprinkled with chopped parsley. Makes 16.

Mushroom Caviar

A delectable stand-in for caviar of the sea.

1/4 cup butter

1/2 lb. mixed fresh wild mushrooms, coarsely chopped

2 tablespoons minced onion

2 tablespoons lemon juice

1 tablespoon Worcestershire sauce

2 tablespoons mayonnaise

Salt and freshly ground pepper to taste

Toast

In a medium skillet melt butter and sauté mushrooms over medium-high heat for 5 minutes. Add minced onion and cook 5 minutes longer. Remove from heat and cool slightly. Drain and place in blender with lemon juice, Worcestershire sauce and mayonnaise. Pulse to a blended but coarse texture. Add salt and pepper to taste. Chill and serve with toast points. Makes 1 cup.

Grow your own mushrooms at home! A peek into Rita's shower might reveal a tower of oysters or a log of shiitakes usurping the space.

Mushroom-Cheese Spread

A quick spread for crackers or baguette slices to serve with a salad, or as a prelude to dinner.

2 cups water

1/2 lb. mixed fresh wild mushrooms

8 oz. cream cheese, room temperature

1/4 teaspoon garlic powder

1 tablespoon butter

Salt and freshly ground pepper to taste

Bring 2 cups water to a boil, drop in mushrooms and blanch for 3 minutes. Drain on a cloth towel. In a food processor, blend cream cheese, garlic powder, butter and mushrooms until smooth. Season with salt and pepper to taste. Makes 1 cup.

Oyster and
Wild Mushroom Appetizer

Another recipe for your scallop shells.
Serve with sliced baguettes and
your guests won't leave a morsel
nor a drop of juice.

2 tablespoons butter

2 cloves garlic, minced

1 pt. oysters, liquid reserved

1/4 cup dry white wine

1 oz. dried mushrooms,
    soaked and chopped or
    1 lb. fresh mushrooms,
    chopped

2 teaspoons ground cumin

2 teaspoons soy sauce

1/2 cup toasted breadcrumbs

2 teaspoons red bell pepper or
    seeded chopped tomato for
    garnish

Baguette, sliced

Preheat oven to 400F (200C). In a large skillet, melt butter and
sauté garlic over medium heat until golden. Add oysters and
sauté 1 minute or until edges curl. Add wine, mushrooms, reserved
oyster liquid and cumin. Reduce heat to low and continue cooking
for 3 minutes. Drizzle with soy sauce. Place 3 oysters in individual
scallop shells or ramekins with some of the juices, top with breadcrumbs and red bell pepper or tomato garnish. Place in oven and
bake about 7 minutes until crumbs are golden brown and crisp.
Serve with sliced baguette. Serves 4.

Pan-fried Mushroom Cap

Commonly known as the parasol mushroom, *lepiota is one of the most flavorful. While it is a perfect choice for this appetizer, portobellos are a fine stand-in.*

1 large mushroom cap

1 whole egg

4 tablespoons cream

Salt and pepper to taste

6 tablespoons butter

1 cup fresh breadcrumbs

Do not wash the mushroom. Cut off the stem and discard it. Brush off the hairlike surface of the cap. In a shallow dish, blend together the egg and cream; season with salt and pepper. In a skillet, heat butter over medium-high heat until it is foamy. Dip the mushroom in egg mixture, cover with breadcrumbs and pat firmly to attach. Fry in butter on both sides until browned. Depending on the size of the mushroom, it will take approximately 5 minutes per side. Cut into wedges to serve. Serves 4.

Remember—mushrooms are very slow to burn because they hold so much moisture. You will find this recipe both meaty and satisfying.

Porcini Tapenade

For a party or for a first course, this tangy porcini mushroom spread is wonderful with baguette slices or buttery little croissants.

6 tablespoons olive oil

1 oz. soaked dried mushrooms, chopped

2 garlic cloves, chopped

2 tablespoons fines herbes

1-1/3 cups dry red wine

18 Kalamata olives, pitted

2 tablespoons capers

1 teaspoon anchovy paste

1-1/2 tablespoons lemon juice

Salt and pepper to taste

Heat 3 tablespoons oil in large skillet and add mushrooms, garlic and fines herbes. Sauté 5 minutes. Add wine, reduce heat. Simmer uncovered until liquid has evaporated. Cool. Transfer to food processor and pulse while adding olives, capers, anchovy paste, lemon juice and remaining 3 tablespoons olive oil. Do not over-blend. Tapenade should have a coarse and hearty texture. Taste for seasoning, adding salt and pepper as desired. Cover and chill. Make one day ahead so flavors will blend. Makes 1 cup.

Sensory Experience: An encounter with a wild mushroom is a sensory experience. The touch of cool flesh, the scent of fresh earth, the color, the form all whisper secrets of the forest as your hands transform fungus to feast.

Rice-paper Chicken with Shiitake Mushrooms

Crispy little packets bursting with flavor are party favorites.

4 dried shiitake mushrooms, soaked, drained, stems removed*

1 (4 oz.) pkg. rice-paper wrappers*

3 tablespoons soy sauce

1 tablespoon dry white wine

1 teaspoon sugar

2 tablespoons sesame oil

1 lb. skinless boneless chicken breast

1/4 lb. ham

1 cup chopped Italian parsley

1 teaspoon five-spice powder*

2 cups oil for frying

Hot Chinese mustard

Soak mushrooms in water to cover; when softened, drain and chop. Soak rice paper in water. Prepare marinade by mixing soy sauce, wine, sugar and sesame oil. Reserve. Slice chicken, ham and mushrooms into julienne strips and mix with parsley and five-spice powder. Put into marinade. In wok heat oil for frying to 300F (150C). On each soft rice-paper wrapper place a spoonful of chicken mixture and wrap like an envelope, folding left corner to right over filling and tucking the remaining corner inside to secure. Fry packages in hot oil about 2 minutes or until lightly browned. Drain and serve with hot Chinese mustard. Makes 20.

* Dried shiitakes, rice paper wrappers and five-spice powder may be found in Asian food sections of your market or specialty stores. Dried shiitakes are sometimes labeled Asian or black Asian mountain mushrooms.

3-Mushroom Toast

A crunchy base with a succulent 3-mushroom topping. Chanterelles, shiitake and enoki are an interesting and delicious combination.

4 tablespoons unsalted butter

1 baguette, sliced

1 medium shallot, finely chopped

4 medium chanterelles, stemmed and cut into fine julienne strips

4 medium shiitake mushrooms, stemmed and cut into fine julienne strips

1/3 cup enoki mushrooms

1/2 cup whipping cream

1/4 cup finely chopped parsley leaves

Salt and freshly ground pepper to taste

Preheat oven to 350F (175C). In a large skillet melt 1 tablespoon butter and brush on the bread slices. Toast on a baking sheet until golden. In the same skillet over low heat, melt 1 tablespoon butter and cook the shallot about 3 minutes until tender. Increase heat to high, add remaining butter and the chanterelle and shiitake mushrooms; sauté quickly for 2 minutes. Reduce heat to low, add the enoki mushrooms and cream. Cook about 2 minutes, stirring constantly until thickened. Stir in the parsley, salt and pepper to taste. Spoon 1 heaping teaspoon mixture on each toast slice. Makes 22.

Wild Mushroom Paté

This sophisticated little appetizer melds texture and taste. It is both crunchy and meaty. You'll serve it again and again as an hors d'oeuvre.

1/2 lb. fresh mushrooms or 1/2 oz. dried wild mushrooms

2/3 cup dry white wine

1/2 lb. butter

10 to 12 chopped green onions, white part only

5 garlic cloves

8 oz. almonds, ground

1/2 teaspoon each dried rosemary and oregano leaves

1/2 teaspoon cumin powder

1 teaspoon dry mustard

1 teaspoon sugar

1/2 cup toasted breadcrumbs

Salt and pepper to taste

French bread, sliced

Finely chop fresh mushrooms or soak dried mushrooms in wine for 20 minutes until soft. Drain wine into a skillet, chop mushrooms and add to skillet, bring to boil over medium heat and cook until liquid has almost evaporated. Remove and set aside. In same skillet, melt 1/4 lb. butter over medium heat, add onions, garlic, almonds, rosemary, oregano, cumin, mustard, sugar and breadcrumbs. Add salt and pepper to taste. Sauté for 5 minutes. Put remaining 1/4 lb. butter into food processor and add skillet mixture. Blend until smooth. Line a two-cup mold with plastic wrap and pack with mushroom mixture. Cover and refrigerate 24 hours. Serve with sliced French bread. Makes 2 cups.

Wild Mushroom Rolls

Wonderful to make ahead and have in your freezer.

1/2 lb. butter

1 lb. mushrooms, finely chopped

6 tablespoons flour

1-1/2 teaspoons salt

2 cups half-and-half

1 teaspoon lemon juice

1 teaspoon onion salt

1-1/2 loaves sliced white sandwich bread

4 tablespoons melted butter

Preheat oven to 400 (205C). In a large skillet, melt 1/2 cup butter over medium-high heat and sauté mushrooms for 5 minutes. Remove from heat and cool slightly. Add flour, blend well. Add salt, stir in half-and-half and cook, stirring constantly until thickened. Stir in lemon juice and onion salt. Cool. Remove crusts from bread slices and with rolling pin, roll very thin. Spread 1 teaspoon or more of mushroom mixture on each slice of flattened bread and roll into a cylinder. Place on a baking sheet, seam side down. Place in freezer about 10 minutes until firm. At this point, you may wrap the rolls in freezer wrap and freeze. To continue, cut rolls into thirds, brush with melted butter and bake 15 to 20 minutes until lightly toasted. Makes 7 or 8 dozen.

Wild Mushroom Spread

One day when you have a minute, make up this quick and succulent spread to have in the freezer for impromptu entertaining.

1/3 cup dried mushrooms, soaked and drained, liquid reserved

2/3 cup water

5 tablespoons unsalted butter

2 green onions, thinly sliced

1/2 cup dry white wine

1 teaspoon Worcestershire sauce

Salt and pepper to taste

Garlic-toasted baguette slices

Soak mushrooms in 2/3 cup water; drain and reserve liquid. In a large sauté pan melt 1 tablespoon butter, sauté onions with wine, mushrooms and soaking liquid for about 10 minutes until tender. Transfer mushrooms to a plate. Reduce liquid to half, about 1/4 cup. When mushrooms are cool, mince them with the onions, add pan liquid and mix with 4 tablespoons unsalted butter, Worcestershire sauce and salt and pepper to taste. Serve with garlic-toasted baguette slices. Makes 1 cup.

As Rita Tells It . . .

An unwise taste-test

As I walked past a well-groomed lawn en route to an elegant reception, I spotted a single purple-grey mushroom. I was just beginning to strike out on my own mushroom quests, and until that day always had an experienced guide to advise me. However, this was a mushroom whose like I had never seen. Its beauty beckoned me and I could not resist it. So I nibbled . . . then nibbled again, for it was quite tasty.

It was a beautiful afternoon, and guests mingled on the lawn, chatting and laughing, grazing on various delicacies, including mushrooms stuffed with duck liver.

When time came and we queued up for the festive buffet, there it was . . . waves of hot and cold swept me and my heart pounded. I looked for a private place away from the crowd, telling myself not to panic, for deep down, I knew . . .

Unlike me to swoon, I swooned away, rousing to hear shouts for a doctor. In minutes five doctors surrounded me. Weak as I was, I managed to say, "It's the mushroom," only to hear a groan, "no-o-o-o, no-o-o-o-o," the host mistaking my purple mushroom for the delicious hors d'oeuvre that had been consumed by 350 guests.

Soon I revived to explain my attack, reassure the host, coming away humbled, having learned not to let my curiosity get the better of me.

As for you, reader, let my experience do it for you, and don't taste until you've identified a mushroom as *edible*.

Soups

Black Forest Soup

*A simple soup that is flavored
with a touch of wine.*

1/2 oz. dried porcini
  mushrooms

1-1/2 tablespoons butter

1 medium onion, finely
  chopped

1 garlic clove, minced

1 tablespoon flour

4 cups water

2 cups milk

Salt and pepper to taste

1 tablespoon port or Madeira
  wine

2 tablespoons finely chopped
  Italian parsley

Soak mushrooms in 1 cup water for 2 to 3 hours. Strain and reserve
liquid. In a small skillet melt butter and sauté onion and garlic over
medium-high heat. Chop mushrooms and add to pan with onion.
Sprinkle with 1 tablespoon flour and stir until smooth. Add water,
reserved liquid and milk. Mix with a wire whisk. Bring to a boil,
reduce heat, cover and simmer for 15 minutes over low heat. Season
with salt and pepper to taste, add the port or Madeira. Garnish with
chopped parsley. Serves 4.

Blewit Crème Soup

A luscious creamy soup from California grape country. A wonderful soup course or light luncheon. Serve with a fine Chardonnay and good French bread.

1 tablespoon butter

1 tablespoon shallots, minced

1 cup blewit mushrooms, thinly sliced

1 cup half-and-half

1 cup chicken stock, page 29

1 teaspoon Pernod

Salt and pepper to taste

2 egg yolks

1/4 cup cream

In a large skillet melt butter and sauté shallots over medium heat, add mushrooms and cook about 2 minutes until mushrooms release their liquids. Add half-and-half, stock, Pernod and salt and pepper to taste. Mix egg yolks with 1/4 cup cream and slowly add to pan mixture, stirring constantly until thickened. Remove from heat and let sit about 5 minutes. Stir again and serve. Serves 4.

Blewits, Clitocybe nuda, are aesthetically pleasing mushrooms, their color light blue to violet, both cap and gills. Their taste is subtle.

Catalan Mushroom Soup

Bolete mushrooms, oil, garlic, onion and tomatoes produce a soup that will enchant those at your table.

2 tablespoons olive oil

2 medium onions, finely chopped

2 garlic cloves, minced

2 tomatoes, peeled, seeded and chopped

2 lbs. fresh mushrooms or 2 oz. soaked dried mushrooms

4 cups chicken, beef or vegetable stock

Salt and pepper to taste

4 slices bread, brushed with olive oil and toasted or grilled

4 sprigs fresh cilantro, chopped

In Dutch oven or 3-quart saucepan heat oil and sauté onions and garlic. Add chopped tomatoes and cook to sauce consistency. Clean mushrooms, cut larger ones in halves or quarters. Add mushrooms to sauce, cover and simmer over low heat 15 to 20 minutes until mushrooms begin to release their liquids. Uncover, add stock, bring to boil. Turn heat to low and simmer uncovered 10 minutes. Add salt and pepper to taste. Place bread in individual soup bowls, pour soup over bread, sprinkle with cilantro. Serves 4.

Mushroom Soup Royale with Boletes

A rich consommé goes royal when flavored with Calvados and crowned with a fancy custard float. A crown cutout would be ever so regal.

2 oz. dried boletes soaked, drained, liquid reserved

2-1/3 cups each chicken and meat stock, pages 29 and 31

1/4 cup Calvados (apple brandy)

Custard cutouts, below

2 tablespoons minced Italian parsley

4 very thin slices of truffle, optional

Chop mushrooms and combine with stock in medium saucepan. Simmer 1 hour. Stir in Calvados. Set aside.

Custard Cutouts

1 egg	1/4 teaspoon salt
1 egg yolk	1/4 teaspoon nutmeg
2 tablespoons milk	Fresh ground pepper to taste

To make custard cutouts: Preheat oven to 325F (165C). Butter a shallow ovenproof dish. In a small bowl, beat egg and egg yolk. Add milk, salt, nutmeg and pepper. Pour mixture into prepared dish, set dish in a bain marie or pan containing hot water about 1 inch deep. Bake 20 to 30 minutes or until custard is set and an inserted knife comes out clean. When completely cool, cut into desired shapes. Cover and refrigerate until ready to use.

To serve, place custard pieces in individual bowls and fill with soup. Custard will float. Garnish with parsley or a slice of truffle. Serves 4.

Ligurian Porcini Soup

This is the way comforting chicken soup is prepared in northern Italy.

1/2 lb. fresh porcini mushrooms or 1/2 oz. dried and
   soaked
6 cups chicken stock, page 29
1/2 lb. angel hair pasta or
   taglierini
Salt and pepper to taste
2 tablespoons chopped Italian
   parsley

Cut fresh or soaked mushrooms into thin strips. In a large pot, bring stock to a boil and add mushrooms. As soon as it returns to a boil, add pasta and cook until al dente. Add salt and pepper to taste. Sprinkle with parsley. Serves 4.

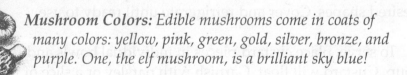

Mushroom Colors: Edible mushrooms come in coats of many colors: yellow, pink, green, gold, silver, bronze, and purple. One, the elf mushroom, is a brilliant sky blue!

Chicken Stock

Once you've tasted your own stock, canned ones will not measure up.

2 tablespoons vegetable oil

5 lbs. chicken wings and backs

2 garlic cloves, sliced

2 large onions, coarsely chopped

2 carrots cut into bite size pieces

4 stalks celery with leaves, chopped

1 small turnip, coarsely chopped

6 quarts water

1/4 cup chopped parsley

1 tablespoon kosher salt

5 whole peppercorns

In a Dutch oven, heat oil and brown chicken pieces with garlic and onion until lightly browned. Add carrots, celery and turnip. Cook about 5 minutes until vegetables have softened, adding a little of the water if pan dries out. Do not let vegetables brown. Add water, parsley, salt and pepper. Bring to a boil. Skim off foam and discard. Reduce heat to low and simmer about 4 hours. Strain, let cool and refrigerate until fat has solidified on top. Remove and discard fat. Refrigerate up to 5 days, or freeze for later use. Makes 8 quarts.

NOTE: To clarify stock, crush an eggshell and mix with 1 egg white and 1/4 cup water. Stir into hot stock and bring to a boil. Let stand 5 minutes, then strain.

Morel Mushroom Soup

Rich and creamy is a soup from the mysterious morel. A slice of crusty bread is a delicious contrasting texture.

2 oz. dried morels

2 cups milk

1 tablespoon butter or oil

2 tablespoons finely chopped onion

2 cloves garlic, finely chopped

6 cups meat stock, page 31 or bouillon cubes may be substituted

2 teaspoons sugar

Salt and white pepper to taste

3 teaspoons Madeira or port wine

3 tablespoons cornstarch

1/2 cup cold water

1 cup cream

1/4 cup dairy sour cream

2 teaspoons chives, chopped for garnish

Soak morels in milk; strain and reserve liquid. Coarsely chop mushrooms. In large skillet heat butter or oil and sauté onion and garlic 2 to 3 minutes until soft. Mix in stock, mushrooms, sugar, salt, pepper and wine. Simmer 20 minutes. Dissolve cornstarch in water and stir into strained soaking liquid. Slowly add to skillet, stirring constantly. Cook until slightly thickened. Add cream and sour cream and taste for seasoning. Top with chopped chives. Serves 4.

Meat Stock

Freeze meat stock in 2-cup containers for future use.

2-1/2 lbs. meaty bones: beef, lamb or game

2 lbs. meaty veal knuckle

2 tablespoons oil

2 carrots

2 leeks, rinsed, chopped

2 stalks celery with leaves, chopped

2 medium onions, chopped

2 cloves garlic, chopped

1 tablespoon fresh thyme or 1/2 teaspoon dried thyme leaves

6 quarts water

6 black peppercorns

1 tablespoon kosher salt

Preheat oven to 425F (220C). In a 13 x 9-inch baking pan place the bones; bake 30 minutes until browned. In a large skillet, heat oil and sauté carrots, leeks, celery, onions, garlic and thyme about 5 minutes until golden. In a large stock pot, place the browned bones and the vegetables. Add water, peppercorns and salt, bring to a boil. Skim off foam and discard. Immediately reduce heat to low, cover and simmer for 4 hours. Cool and place in refrigerator. When fat has solidified on top, remove and discard it. Strain the stock. Store in refrigerator for 5 days, or freeze for later use. Makes 8 quarts.

As Rita Tells It

Up and Over from Down Under

It was the first day of school vacation in Hamilton, a small town on the north island of New Zealand. Fall had colored the trees in rich shades of gold and crimson, while the meadows had soaked up recent rains and turned to emerald green. My host, Bryan Mayall, lives across from the school rugby field which has seen the daily rough and tumble of children's sport. But the athletic shoes had moved out that day, allowing for a leisurely stroll. There overnight the ground released what would be my welcoming committee: Dozens of Agaricus campestri to fill Bryan's basket as a gift for my arrival. Thank you, Bryan! And thank you, young sportsmen for taking another road and allowing the emergence of ingredients for Satin Soup!

Satin Soup

The very essence of joy and comfort food. Agaricus campestri is a wonderful choice.

1 lb. fresh wild mushrooms

1/2 cup flour

2 tablespoons butter

2 cups milk

1 cup cream

Salt and pepper to taste

4 drops onion juice

1/4 cup minced Italian parsley

Chop mushrooms, place in small plastic bag with flour and shake to coat mushrooms. In large sauté pan melt butter over medium heat and sauté mushrooms about 5 minutes until tender, but not browned. Slowly stir in milk and cream. Season with salt, pepper and onion juice. Sprinkle with minced parsley. Serves 6.

Cooking will tame the wild mushrooms, but do not eat a raw one. Digestional upset will be the price you pay.

Thai Flowered Chicken Soup

A true cup of grace, this lovely soup has a floating meringue island studded with a dramatic black mushroom flower.

4 dried shiitake mushrooms, soaked, stems removed, liquid reserved*

1 boneless, skinless, chicken breast, about 1 lb.

1/2 teaspoon salt

1 tablespoon dry white wine

1 cup shelled shrimp

4 egg whites, divided

Salt

2 teaspoons cornstarch

5 cups chicken stock, page 29

Salt and pepper to taste

1 tablespoon chopped cilantro

Thai hot sauce to taste

Soak mushrooms in 1/2 cup water; drain and reserve liquid. In a small bowl, marinate chicken breast in 1/2 teaspoon salt and 1 tablespoon white wine 15 minutes. Meanwhile slice each soaked mushroom into 4 even pieces. In small skillet over medium-high heat pour 1/4 cup soaking liquid, add mushrooms and cook about 3 minutes until tender. Remove from pan and set aside. Preheat oven to 400F (200C). In food processor, mince shrimp with 1 egg white, a pinch of salt and the cornstarch. Place marinated chicken breast in baking dish and spread with all the shrimp mixture, smoothing the top. Bake for 15 minutes. Serves 4.

Remove chicken and cut into four diamond-shaped pieces. Turn oven to 450F (220C). In a small bowl beat remaining egg whites very stiff and spoon onto a baking sheet in four mounds, smoothing the tops. Decorate each with mushroom slices and bake in oven for 3 minutes. Meanwhile, place chicken diamonds into 4 soup bowls and cover with hot soup stock seasoned with salt and pepper to taste. Slip one egg-white mound into each bowl on top of soup. Sprinkle with cilantro and few drops of Thai hot sauce, if desired. Serves 4.

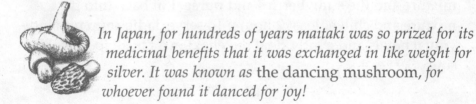

In Japan, for hundreds of years maitaki was so prized for its medicinal benefits that it was exchanged in like weight for silver. It was known as the dancing mushroom, *for whoever found it danced for joy!*

* Dried shiitakes may be found in Asian food sections of your market or in specialty stores. Dried shiitakes are sometimes labeled Asian or black Asian mountain mushrooms.

Chilled Fruit Soup with Strawberry and Enoki Mushrooms

Pretty as an Easter bonnet, this cool, fresh soup features a flotilla of slender enoki mushrooms.

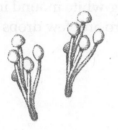

4 cups chicken bouillon or bouillon cubes

1 inner stalk of celery, chopped

1 teaspoon dried mint

1 level tablespoon sugar

1 small carrot, peeled and chopped

2 cups Burgundy wine

1 quart ripe strawberries, washed and hulled

1 bundle enoki mushrooms

In a 3-quart saucepan combine bouillon, celery, mint, sugar, carrot and wine. Bring to a boil, reduce to low and simmer covered for 20 minutes. Cool. Strain through a fine sieve and discard vegetables. In a blender combine 1 cup of the bouillon mixture and the strawberries and purée. Put back into the mixture and chill at least 2 hours. To serve, ladle soup into individual bowls and gently float the enoki in a fan shape atop the soup. Serves 4.

Theo's Soup

*Caps of puff pastry top this
rich and delicious soup.
Spoon through the cap to reach the
sumptuous soup.*

3 cups water

2 oz. dried morels

2 tablespoons melted butter

1 tablespoon chopped red or
yellow pepper

1 tablespoon finely chopped
onion

2 teaspoons salt

1 teaspoon sugar

2 tablespoons soy sauce

1 egg, lightly beaten

4 (4-inch) squares frozen
puff pastry, thawed

In a small saucepan bring water to a boil and drop in mushrooms,
reduce heat and simmer for 30 minutes. Reserve liquid. In a large
skillet, melt butter over medium heat and cook the pepper and
onion until soft. Add the mushrooms and their liquid, salt, sugar
and soy sauce. Bring back to simmer. Remove from heat.

To make pastry caps, roll out 4 pastry squares with a rolling
pin until thin and trim into rounds that will cover and lap over
the rims of 4 ovenproof serving cups. Brush beaten egg in a 2-inch-
wide band around the top outside edge of each pastry. Pour in the
soup and cover with the pastry, lapping it over and sealing it to the
egg-coated rim. Refrigerate 1 hour or more.

Preheat oven to 450F (235C). Remove cups from refrigerator,
let come to room temperature. Bake 5 to 7 minutes until pastry is
golden brown. Serves 4.

Consommé with Truffle Ravioli

The secret tucked inside these succulent ravioli is truffle! Use the finest consommé you can make or buy.

Ravioli dough, below

2 tablespoons butter

1 leek, white part only, cut in 1-inch julienne

2 truffles, cut in small strips

1 teaspoon cognac

5 cups consommé

Prepare ravioli dough or thaw frozen ravioli dough. Melt butter in medium skillet over medium heat. Add leek julienne and sauté until soft. Add truffles and cognac. Cook for 2 minutes.

To assemble: Roll dough into a thin sheet 12 x 6 inches. Cut into eight 3-inch squares. Place 1 teaspoon truffle filling on each square; fold over into triangles, sealing water-dampened edges with your fingers. Cover with damp towel until ready to cook. Bring consommé to a boil and drop in ravioli, simmering until they rise to the top. Serve with 2 ravioli in each bowl. Serves 4.

Ravioli Dough

1 3/4 cup all-purpose flour

1/4 teaspoon salt

2 eggs

On a work surface, sift flour with salt into a mound, make a well in the center and add eggs. Work into a soft dough, form into a ball, wrap in plastic and let it rest while you prepare the filling.

Wild Mushroom Vichyssoise

*Mushrooms give jaunty new character
to this French classic.*

1/2 oz. dried morels or any
   dried mushroom, soaked,
   liquid reserved
2 potatoes, peeled, diced
2 cups water plus water to boil
   potatoes
1 leek, rinsed and finely
   chopped
2 tablespoons finely chopped
   onion

1 teaspoon salt
1 teaspoon sugar
1 tablespoon tamari sauce
1 cup whipping cream
Milk to thin, if necessary
1 leek, finely chopped, white
   part only

Soak mushrooms in 1-1/2 cups water; drain and reserve liquid. In a
1-quart saucepan boil the potatoes in 2 inches water until tender. In
a 3-quart saucepan combine 2 cups water with mushrooms, 1/2 of
the chopped leek, onions, salt, sugar and tamari sauce. Bring to a
boil, then reduce heat and simmer until liquid is reduced to 1 cup.
Remove vegetables and purée in a food processor. Mix
cream and mushroom soaking liquid into the liquid
in the saucepan. Add the mushroom purée and
blend well. Add milk if soup is too thick.
Refrigerate until chilled. Top with remaining
chopped leek. Serves 4.

Curry Vegetable Soup

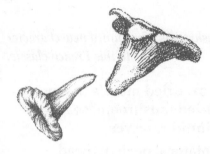

With mushrooms like chanterelles, who needs meat? This is a hearty soup to serve with peasant bread or cornbread. A glass of red wine and a fruit tart for dessert and you have a delicious, wholesome meal.

3 tablespoons olive oil

1/2 onion, finely chopped

1 garlic clove, minced

3 cardamom seeds, crushed

1 teaspoon curry paste or powder

1 pinch saffron, crumbled

1 cup red potatoes, peeled, diced

1/2 cup baby okra

1/2 lb. mushrooms

1/4 lb. chanterelles or black trumpets

4 cups chicken stock, page 29, or vegetable broth

1 egg yolk

Salt and pepper to taste

2 tablespoons fresh mint, chopped for garnish

In 3-quart saucepan, heat oil over medium heat. Add onion, garlic, cardamom, curry, saffron, potatoes and okra and cook until onion is transparent, about 2 minutes. Cover and cook over low heat for 20 minutes. Add mushrooms and broth, bring quickly to a boil, reduce heat and simmer 25 minutes. In a small bowl, beat the egg yolk. Very slowly add 1/2 cup of the hot soup to the beaten yolk, stirring constantly to prevent yolk from curdling. Stir until well mixed and cooled. Stir egg yolk into soup and garnish with mint. Serves 4.

Watercress Soup with Morel Mushrooms

Morels take a little extra effort to clean out grit that may hide in their multiple chambers. It is well worth using morels for this soup to enhance the delicacy of the watercress.

1 lb. fresh mushrooms or 1 oz. dried mushrooms, soaked, drained

5 tablespoons butter

1 teaspoon lemon juice

1/4 teaspoon salt

Pepper to taste

4 cups stemmed, snipped watercress (reserve stems)

1/4 cup minced onion

3 tablespoons flour

4 cups chicken stock, page 29

Chop mushrooms. Melt 3 tablespoons butter in a 3-quart saucepan over medium heat and add mushrooms. Sprinkle with lemon juice, salt and pepper. Cover and cook 10 minutes, stirring occasionally. Set aside. Coarsely chop watercress stems and set aside. In a Dutch oven melt 2 tablespoons butter, add 3-1/2 cups watercress leaves, stems and onion and stir until wilted. Cook 2 minutes and sprinkle with flour, stirring to blend. Set aside 3/4 cup mushrooms. Combine remaining mushrooms with chicken stock and pour into Dutch oven mix, stirring 10 minutes. In 4 batches, pour mixture into blender or food processor and process until smooth. Return soup to pan and add reserved chopped mushrooms. Bring to a boil and serve hot. Garnish with the remaining watercress. Serves 6.

How to Harvest a Spore Print

Pluck a freshly opened mushroom. Pluck out the stem, careful not to disturb fragile gills under the cap.

On a smooth, flat surface like a table, lay cap stem-side down on a blank sheet of paper. Cover the mushroom with a drinking glass to make airtight. Within 8 hours, your mushroom will deposit its unique spore print on the paper.

Rita captures spore prints on a nice quality paper and uses it for note stationery.

On this page and others are spore prints from an Agaricus mushroom that materialized in Rita's yard after a rainfall. Depending on the mushroom, spore prints are not only black, but white, grey, pink and numerous shades of brown.

How to Make Mushroom Paper

At times in Telluride, we fungophiles have found so many mushrooms, both edible and inedible, that in order not to waste their lives, we made beautiful handmade papers in shades of gold and fawn.

Here is a simple recipe: Fill a blender 3/4 full of water. Add 2 sheets of plain paper torn into shreds and a handful of fresh or dried mushroom pieces, or a combination. Blend on high until paper and mushrooms are incorporated. Pour over a piece of fine screen wire and drain. When most of water has drained through, press sponge on top of mixture, absorbing excess water. Press paper into shape of choice, blotting and pressing until it has form. When partially dry and holding its shape, remove from screen and hang to air dry on a clothespin hanger.

You may also cut paper-thin slices of mushroom and press with a sponge into the mixture on the screen, proceeding as above. Try this with colored mushrooms. Makes a sheet of handmade paper about 4 x 6 inches.

Salads

Almost-raw Lactarius Deliciosus Salad

Here's a recipe you might think breaks the rule about always cooking the wild ones—the trick is this: the vinegar is heated and cooks the lactarius when you assemble the salad.

1/2 lb. mushrooms

2/3 cup olive oil

Salt and pepper to taste

1/3 cup rice vinegar

1/4 cup thinly sliced red onion

1/4 teaspoon sugar

6 cups salad greens

1 tablespoon chopped Italian parsley

Cut mushrooms into thin slices. In a medium bowl place mushrooms with the olive oil, salt and pepper. In a small saucepan bring vinegar to a boil and pour over mushroom mixture, add onion and sugar and toss to blend. Cover and refrigerate. Divide greens onto individual plates or put onto a platter; top with mushroom mixture and sprinkle with parsley. Serves 4.

Lactarius deliciosus, *as its Latin name suggests, is a delicious mushroom. When pierced it gives off an orangy-white milk. Because it is fragile and brittle, it is not suitable for drying. It is not yet widely available, so grab it when you see it and make this fantastic salad.*

Artichokes and Mushrooms in Bleu-Cheese Vinaigrette

A winning threesome with mixed greens makes a fabulous salad.

1 tablespoon butter

1/2 lb. mixed mushrooms, finely minced

8 artichoke halves, cooked and hollowed out*

1/2 lb. button mushrooms, marinated

3/4 cup olive oil

1/4 cup bleu cheese, crumbled

1/2 cup red wine vinegar

2 tablespoons lemon juice

Salt

1/2 teaspoon pepper

4 garlic cloves, minced

3 tablespoons minced fresh basil or tarragon

2 cups mixed salad greens

1/2 cup seeded and chopped fresh tomatoes

In a small skillet melt butter and sauté minced mushrooms 2 minutes until tender. Set aside. Cut cooked artichokes in half lengthwise and remove choke. Cool and refrigerate, if desired. Halve or quarter button mushrooms. In a small bowl, combine olive oil and bleu cheese. Add vinegar, lemon juice, salt to taste, pepper, garlic, basil and cooked mushrooms. Toss with cut button mushrooms, cover and refrigerate for 24 hours. To assemble, arrange salad greens on individual plates, place artichoke half on greens and fill cavity with mushroom mixture, drizzling vinaigrette marinade over the top. Garnish with chopped tomatoes. Serves 4.

* Artichokes may be cooked and refrigerated 3 days ahead.

Fusilli and Porcini

An uncommon pasta salad that is rich with mushroom flavor.

1/2 oz. dried porcini mushrooms, soaked

2 tablespoons butter

3 tablespoons vegetable oil

2 teaspoons dark sesame oil

1/4 cup balsamic or red wine vinegar

1 teaspoon soy sauce

1 garlic clove, crushed

8 oz. fusilli pasta, cooked and drained

Salt and freshly ground pepper, to taste

1 tablespoon chopped Italian parsley

Strain soaked mushrooms and reserve liquid. Slice the mushrooms. In a small skillet melt the butter over high heat and sauté the mushrooms about 5 minutes until tender. Set aside. In a small bowl combine 2 tablespoons reserved mushroom liquid, vegetable and sesame oils, vinegar, soy sauce and garlic. Pour over the cooked pasta, add mushrooms and salt and pepper to taste. Toss well and garnish with parsley. Serves 4.

In ancient times patrician Romans so favored the gustatory delights of wild mushrooms that they forbade by law any lower classes from either eating or preparing them. No aristocratic home was without boletaria, *vessels of precious metals made just for preparing mushrooms, which the host did, himself.*

Fennel and Mushroom Salad

Fennel is also known as finocchio, *or* sweet anise. *It has a mild licorice flavor.*

1 oz. dried mushrooms

1 cup dry white wine

3/4 cup sour cream

1 tablespoon caraway seeds

1/4 cup chopped fresh chives

Salt and pepper to taste

2 cups water

2 fresh fennel bulbs

In a medium saucepan boil dried mushrooms in wine for 5 minutes. Drain and dry on paper towels. Slice mushrooms, mix with sour cream, caraway seeds and chives. Refrigerate 2 hours and season with salt and pepper to taste. In a saucepan, bring 2 cups water to a boil, drop in the fennel bulbs for 3 minutes. Cool and slice bulbs crosswise. To serve, arrange a bed of fennel on serving plates or a platter and heap mushrooms on top. Serves 4.

Mushroom-Hazelnut Salad

Mixed packages of fresh wild mushrooms usually include a variety of colorful mushrooms that add interest to this lovely salad.

5 tablespoons olive oil

1 tablespoon balsamic or red wine vinegar

1 tablespoon chopped fresh tarragon or 1 teaspoon dried leaf tarragon

2 garlic cloves, chopped

1/4 teaspoon honey

Salt and pepper to taste

8 oz. fresh mushrooms, sliced

6 cups mixed salad greens

1/3 cup toasted chopped hazelnuts

In a small bowl, whisk together 4 tablespoons oil, vinegar, tarragon, garlic and honey. Season with salt and pepper to taste. This dressing may be prepared 2 hours ahead. Let stand at room temperature until needed. Heat remaining tablespoon oil in a medium skillet over medium-high heat. Add mushrooms and sauté about 5 minutes until tender. Place salad greens in large bowl. Toss with half of dressing. Divide among plates, spoon mushrooms on top of salads, drizzle with remaining dressing and garnish with hazelnuts. Serves 4.

Roasted Pepper and Honey Mushroom Salad

Roast a mix of red, yellow, green, orange and purple peppers for this beautiful dinner salad.

4 bell peppers

2 cups water

1/2 lb. fresh honey mushrooms

2 cups fresh spinach leaves, rinsed and dried

1/4 cup olive oil

2 tablespoons orange-juice concentrate

2 tablespoons vinegar

1 tablespoon thinly sliced red onion

2 tablespoons raw pine nuts

On a shallow baking sheet roast whole bell peppers in 450F (235C) oven, turning until blackened all over. Place in paper bag for 10 minutes, then peel, seed and slice into strips. Set aside. Bring 2 cups water to a boil, drop in mushrooms and blanch for 1 minute. Remove from water with slotted spoon and set aside. Arrange spinach leaves on platter or individual plates. In a medium bowl combine olive oil, orange-juice concentrate, vinegar and onion. Add pepper strips and mushrooms and toss to combine. Pour mixture over spinach and sprinkle with pine nuts. Serves 4.

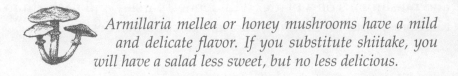

Armillaria mellea or honey mushrooms have a mild and delicate flavor. If you substitute shiitake, you will have a salad less sweet, but no less delicious.

Spinach and Oyster Mushroom Salad

Deep-green spinach with frosty white oyster mushrooms, a dressing of tart lemon and nasturtium blossoms make a picturesque salad.

1 tablespoon olive oil

1/2 lb. fresh oyster mushrooms cut in 1/2-inch pieces

6 cups fresh spinach leaves, washed

1/2 fennel bulb, thinly sliced

1/4 cup coarsely chopped Italian parsley

6 to 12 nasturtium flowers for garnish

Dressing
Juice of 1 lemon

4 tablespoons white wine vinegar

3 tablespoons walnut oil

1/4 cup vegetable oil

Prepare dressing: In a small jar combine dressing ingredients. Cover and shake until mixed.

In a medium skillet heat olive oil and sauté mushrooms about 5 minutes until tender. Add spinach leaves and press down with spatula, cooking about 1 minute until barely wilted. Place spinach and mushrooms on a platter with fennel, parsley and nasturtium blossoms, pour on dressing and toss to combine. Serves 4.

Wild Mushroom Salad with Warm Balsamic Vinaigrette

An outstanding salad to serve at luncheon or as prelude to a fine dinner.

Vinaigrette, below

2 teaspoons olive oil

6 cups mixed wild mushrooms

1 teaspoon salt

Pepper to taste

4 cups mixed greens

Prepare vinaigrette. In a large skillet heat olive oil and sauté mushrooms about 2 minutes until tender. Add salt and pepper to taste. Cool, set aside.

To serve, divide greens among 4 plates, top with mushrooms, spoon warm vinaigrette over all and serve immediately. Serves 4.

Vinaigrette
2 tablespoons olive oil

2 shallots, minced

1 garlic clove, minced

1/4 cup dry white wine

1/4 cup chicken broth

1/4 cup balsamic vinegar

1 tablespoon fresh thyme leaves, chopped

1/2 teaspoon salt

Freshly ground pepper to taste

In a medium skillet heat 1 tablespoon oil. Sauté shallots and garlic 2 minutes until browned. Add wine, chicken broth and vinegar. Simmer until reduced by half, about 10 minutes. Stir in remaining tablespoon oil, thyme, salt and pepper. Serves 4.

Tomato, Basil and Mushroom Salad

With the availability of fresh produce year 'round, you can enjoy this salad anytime.

5 teaspoons olive oil

2 teaspoons balsamic vinegar

1 shallot, minced

1 garlic clove, minced

Salt and pepper to taste

2 oz. fresh oyster mushrooms, sliced into bite-size pieces

2-1/2 oz. fresh shiitake, stems removed, sliced into bite-size pieces

1/4 teaspoon dried marjoram

1 tablespoon wine vinegar

3 tablespoons olive oil

4 medium tomatoes sliced horizontally

12 to 15 whole fresh basil leaves

Salt and pepper to taste

In a small bowl whisk 3 teaspoons oil, vinegar, 1/4 of chopped shallot and 1/4 of the garlic to blend. Add salt and pepper to taste. In a large skillet heat remaining 2 teaspoons oil over medium heat. Add mushrooms. Sauté about 5 minutes. Add marjoram and remaining shallot and garlic. Sauté 5 minutes longer. Remove from heat. In a cup combine 1 tablespoon wine vinegar and 3 tablespoons olive oil. On a large flat platter arrange an overlapping circle of tomato slices with whole basil leaves tucked among them. Sprinkle with vinegar and oil mixture. In the center pile the mushrooms. Season with salt and pepper to taste. Serves 4.

First Courses

Baked Mushroom Caps

*Très élégant, three on a plate—
French bread rounds as a
prelude to dinner.*

1/2 tablespoon butter

Salt and pepper to taste

1/2 teaspoon minced parsley

1/2 teaspoon minced shallots

Juice of half a lemon

1/2 to 1 teaspoon cream

12 slices French bread,
   buttered, toasted, crusts
   trimmed

12 fresh mushroom caps

Preheat oven to 400F (200C). In a medium bowl beat butter, salt,
pepper, parsley, shallots, lemon juice and cream until soft and well
blended. Spread on individual bread slices, place a mushroom,
curved side down, on each and set on a baking dish. Cover and
bake 20 to 25 minutes until mushrooms are tender, but not limp.
Serve immediately. Serves 4.

Baked Oysters Supreme

Land meets shore in this luscious casserole that unites oyster mushrooms and oysters from the sea, two unlikely, but very compatible components.

3 tablespoons butter

1/4 cup oyster or other mushrooms, sliced

4 green onions, chopped

1/2 cup chopped Italian parsley

1 cup breadcrumbs

Salt and pepper to taste

1 pt. oysters, cut in thirds or halves

1 cup dairy sour cream

1/8 teaspoon nutmeg

Preheat oven to 350F (180C). Oil a 4-cup ovenproof casserole. In skillet over medium-high heat, melt butter. Sauté mushrooms with onions, parsley, breadcrumbs, salt and pepper, about 5 minutes. Place a layer of breadcrumb mixture in bottom of casserole, then a layer of oysters. Add a layer of sour cream and nutmeg. Repeat until all ingredients are used, finishing with sour cream. Bake 20 minutes. Serves 4.

Vegetarians' Delight: Vegetarians consider mushrooms the gustatory equivalent of meat, in both texture and ingratiating quality. Indeed, in a dark, rich sauce, their flavor has fooled many a carnivore.

As Rita Tells It

Himalayan Journey

High in the Himalayas, I came upon a patch of mushrooms so blue it looked as if a bit of sky had fallen. *Helvellas!* Elf saddles! What a find! I sat, marveling that such a thing could be, wanting, and not wanting, to pluck them. Of course, a good hunter cannot return to camp without a treasure.

As I sat, savoring the moment, a recipe for elf saddles came like magic into my head, and I thought of brilliant yellow saffron and bright-blue mushrooms over golden strands of angel-hair pasta. I could hardly wait to get back to camp and a stove! There I prepared what I'd seen in my reverie on the mountain, with wild monkeys pounding on the window of our hut.

Elf Saddles over Pasta

Delicate blue mushrooms create a surprising treat.

2 tablespoons oil

2 tablespoons finely minced shallots

1 teaspoon minced garlic

1/2 teaspoon saffron, crumbled

1/2 lb. elf saddles or other mushrooms

1/2 lb. angel hair pasta, cooked, drained and kept warm

In a medium skillet heat the oil over medium-high heat and sauté shallots and garlic 2 minutes until tender. Crumble in saffron, pulverizing between your fingers, add the mushrooms and cook 5 minutes until tender. Pour over cooked angel hair pasta. Serves 4.

Glorious Truffle Omelet

Though many truffle lovers prefer to peel and shave raw truffles over eggs or pasta, here's an omelet that features sautéed truffles.

1 truffle, wiped clean
  and peeled

2 tablespoons unsalted butter

8 eggs

1 tablespoon cream

Salt to taste

Freshly ground pepper to
  taste

Cut 4 slim slices from center of truffle, mince remainder and peelings. Melt 1 tablespoon butter in a small skillet. Add truffle slices and toss to coat. Remove and reserve. Add minced truffle to skillet and toss to coat. Remove and reserve separately. Combine eggs, cream and minced truffle in bowl, stir gently to mix. Do not beat. Melt remaining butter in large non-stick skillet. Pour in egg mixture and stir once or twice with a spoon. Shake pan so eggs cover the bottom, and keep shaking so eggs do not stick or burn. Continue until done to your liking. Fold in half, slide onto platter and garnish with truffle slices. Serve immediately with freshly ground pepper. Serves 4.

Never discard a bit of truffle, except for soft spots. If you do not use all of it, even the peel, there are two ways to preserve it. Place the unused portion in a jar with a tight lid. Fill the jar with brandy, vodka, bourbon or other high-alcohol beverage. Or, place truffle pieces in a jar and pour in high-quality oil to cover pieces, as I often do. The truffle pieces will retain their flavor in solution unless air gets to them.

Grilled
King Bolete

If you are fortunate enough to encounter a King Bolete, bring it home and present it as a stunning first course. Its crown could be as large as 8 or 10 inches in diameter, the bulbous stem as long as 6 inches! This is also a fine accompaniment to steak or chops.

1 giant bolete mushroom
1/4 cup olive oil

Heat your grill to medium high. Slice the bolete lengthwise, crown through stem, into 1/4-inch slabs. Sprinkle with olive oil and grill close to the fire for about 1 minute each side. Serves 4.

Boletus edulis *is available dried in some specialty markets for other applications. You'll need the fresh one for this recipe.*

Because mushrooms contain a lot of water, there is little danger of burning them.

Huitlacoche Quesadillas

A little-known treasure, huitlacoche emerges as a blue-black fungus growing on corn in the fields of Mexico. Don't judge it by its looks, but try it to discover why Mexican gourmets are so fond of it. It is available frozen.

1 tablespoon oil

2 cloves garlic, minced

2 shallots, finely chopped

3/4 cup red bell pepper

1/2 lb. huitlacoche, sliced

1/2 lb. shiitake mushrooms, sliced

Tabasco® sauce to taste

3 tablespoons finely chopped fresh cilantro

Salt and pepper to taste

1 cup grated Monterey Jack cheese

4 oz. goat cheese, crumbled

4 (10-inch) flour tortillas

In a large skillet, heat oil and sauté garlic, shallots and red bell pepper about 3 minutes until tender. Cut huitlacoche and shiitakes into 1/4-inch slices and add to skillet, cooking until liquid evaporates. Season with Tabasco sauce, cilantro, salt and pepper. In a small bowl toss cheeses together and reserve.

Place a tortilla in a non-stick skillet that has been heated over medium heat. Spoon on 1/4 cheese mixture, and 1/4 mushroom mixture. Fold in half with spatula and cook until cheeses begin to melt. Turn and cook until cheeses bubble. Remove from pan and cut into 4 wedges. Repeat with remaining tortillas and ingredients. Serves 4.

Morels Stuffed
with Chicken Mousse

*Your guests will acclaim your skills
when you serve this combination of
flavors and textures.*

4 skinless, boned chicken
    thighs, cut into small pieces
1 whole shallot, peeled
3/4 cup whipping cream
3/4 teaspoon salt
2 teaspoons dried dill
1 teaspoon curry powder
1 shallot, peeled, minced
16 large morels, cleaned and
    sliced in half lengthwise
    (will be hollow)
2 tablespoons unsalted butter

Preheat oven to 350F (180C). Butter a small baking dish. Place
chicken in food processor with the whole shallot and pulse. Scrape
down sides and continue pulsing while slowly adding 1/4 cup
cream. Scrape again and continue, adding another 1/4 cup cream.
Add salt, dill and curry powder; pulse until the consistency of
whipped cream.

In a small saucepan, combine the minced shallot with the
remaining cream. Cook over low heat 2 minutes, but do not boil.
Set aside. Using a spoon or pastry bag, stuff morels with chicken
mixture, and place in baking dish. Pour on the cream sauce, cover
and bake 10 minutes. Baste with pan liquids and cook 5 minutes
more. Melt 2 tablespoons butter and pour over the mushrooms.
On individual serving plates place a dollop of sauce. Place morels
on top, 2 per plate. Serves 8.

Mushroom Fritatta

Here is a simple, yet delicious Italian omelet.

3 tablespoons olive oil

5 green onions, finely chopped, white part only

2 cups mixed wild mushrooms

Salt and pepper to taste

6 eggs, well beaten

1/4 cup Parmesan cheese

3 tablespoons finely chopped cilantro

Coat a 10-inch heatproof platter with 1 tablespoon oil and set aside. In a 10-inch omelet pan pour remaining 2 tablespoons oil. Over medium heat sauté onions for 1 minute. Add mushrooms, salt and pepper. Turn heat to medium high and cook 5 minutes. Add eggs. Do not stir. Cook until top looks creamy and the edges begin to set. Remove from heat. Turn oven to broil. Invert oiled ovenproof platter over the omelet pan and transfer the fritatta onto the platter. Place under broiler for 1 minute, sprinkle with Parmesan cheese and cilantro. Serves 4.

Oldest Mushroom? Guess what the 5000-year-old ice man was wearing when a melting glacier exposed him in 1991. The frozen remains of the oldest, best-preserved human body ever recovered was wearing two mushrooms *on a cord around his neck! . . . The assumption is that they were to be used for medicinal purposes as he set out on some errand high in the Alps along the Austrian-Italian border.*

Pasta
with White Truffles

Unmistakable—the flavor and aroma of truffle in this simple pasta dish. Keep accompanying courses subtle— a simple broth, steamed vegetables and crunchy French bread. And, of course, a fine wine.

1 large white truffle, about 2 to 3 oz.

1/2 cup crème fraîche, below

4 tablespoons unsalted butter

Salt and freshly ground pepper to taste

Angel hair pasta, cooked

Wipe truffle with damp cloth or brush. Shave about 1/4 of truffle with sharp paring knife or vegetable peeler and reserve. Slice remainder as thinly as possible. In a small saucepan, combine crème fraîche, butter and truffle slices. Cook over medium heat until cream is reduced by half. Season with salt and pepper. Pour sauce over the hot pasta, toss and sprinkle with shaved truffle. Serve immediately. Serves 4.

Crème Fraîche
1 pt. heavy cream
4 tablespoons buttermilk

Combine in a quart jar, cover tightly and shake vigorously 1 minute. Set in a warm place for 48 to 72 hours. When about as thick as sour cream, refrigerate. It will keep about 3 weeks.

Other Uses for Crème Fraîche: Topping for soups or baked desserts. Use as you would sour cream, whipped sweet cream or yogurt.

Puff Pastry Squares with Morel Cream Sauce

Crisp puff pastry, topped with a mushroom cream sauce. If morels are not readily available, substitute shiitake.

1-1/2 cups hot water

1 cup Madeira wine

3 oz. dried morels or shiitake

1/2 pkg. (17-1/4 oz.) frozen puff pastry, thawed

2 cups whipping cream

Salt and freshly ground pepper to taste

Cayenne pepper to taste

In a medium bowl, pour hot water and Madeira over mushrooms and let stand 2 hours at room temperature. Line sieve with 3 layers of dampened cheesecloth; place over small saucepan. Strain mushroom-soaking liquid through cheesecloth. If using shiitake, trim off stems and discard. Cut mushrooms lengthwise into 1/4-inch slices. Add to liquid in saucepan and boil until liquid is reduced to 1/2 cup. To this point recipe may be prepared a day ahead. Cover and refrigerate.

To continue, preheat oven to 425F (220C). Cut pastry into four 4-inch squares. Place on large baking sheet, spacing evenly. Bake until golden, about 10 minutes. Cool slightly on rack. Cut tops from pastry squares, place bottoms on 4 plates. Bring mushroom mixture to room temperature. Boil cream until reduced to 1 cup. Add to mushroom mixture. Season with salt, pepper and cayenne. Bring to boil, stirring constantly. Spoon over pastries, replace tops. Serves 4.

Porcini Soufflé with Cream Sauce

An unforgettably elegant first course.

Cream Sauce, next page

1 oz. dried mushrooms

1 cup dry white wine

2 cups milk, scalded

4 tablespoons butter

2/3 cup flour

6 egg yolks, room temperature

1 cup cheese

5 egg whites, room temperature

1/4 teaspoon salt

In a bowl, soak mushrooms in wine, set aside. Preheat oven to 350F (175C). Butter 6 ramekins or an 8-inch soufflé dish. Cut a collar of waxed paper or parchment 2 inches longer than the circumference of your dish and 2 inches taller. Butter one side of paper and press buttered side to outside of dish, overlap and tie a length of string around the collar to secure it. Drain mushrooms, strain and use soaking liquid to make cream sauce. Cool scalded milk to lukewarm.

In medium saucepan, melt butter, stir in flour, whisking over medium heat until smooth. Slowly add milk, whisking briskly, remove from heat and cool. Beat in egg yolks, mushrooms and cheese. Mix thoroughly. To this point, recipe may be made ahead.

To continue, beat egg whites with salt until stiff. Fold into sauce gently and thoroughly. Spoon into buttered, collared soufflé dish. Bake in water bath (set dishes in pan with water about halfway up the sides) in preheated oven for 45 minutes. Test for doneness with a wooden pick. Serve with Cream Sauce. Serves 6.

Cream Sauce

Mushroom soaking liquid
1 cup whipping cream
Salt and pepper to taste

Heat mushroom soaking liquid in a saucepan over medium-high heat; add cream and reduce by half. Adjust seasoning, with salt and pepper to taste.

If you are using a soufflé dish, after filling it with the ingredients, you may immediately put it in the freezer! In preparation for serving, place the frozen soufflé into a pre-heated 325F (160C) oven and bake 1 hour, or until it rises. Serve immediately.

Radicchio Cups with Wild Mushrooms

The rich wine color and unique texture of radicchio complements the mushroom filling.

5 tablespoons olive oil

1/2 lb. fresh mixed wild mushrooms, cut in bite-size pieces

Salt and pepper to taste

3 tablespoons chopped fresh parsley

1/4 cup whipping cream

16 fresh radicchio or butter lettuce cups, rinsed and drained

In a medium skillet heat oil and sauté mushrooms over medium-high heat 2 to 3 minutes until tender. Add salt and pepper to taste. Lower heat, stir in parsley and cream and bring to a simmer. Remove from heat. Spoon into radicchio cups and serve 4 to a person. Serves 4.

Mushrooms are our nutritional friends.

2/3 cup of whole wild mushrooms (2 oz.) contains:

Food Energy	14 calories	Vitamin A*	
Carbohydrate	2 g	Vitamin C*	
Fat	1/2 g	Vitamin B6*	
Protein	1 g	Potassium	140 mg
Crude Fiber	200 mg	Sodium	3 mg
Riboflavin	10%	Copper	6%
Niacin	8%	Phosphorus	4%
Pantothenic Acid	4%	Calcium*	
Thiamin	2%	Iron*	
Cholesterol	0 mg		

*contains less than 2% USRDA requirement

Stuffed Bolete Caps

Two on a plate is a substantial, handsome first course.

8 fresh bolete caps

5 heaping tablespoons breadcrumbs

1 tablespoon shredded Swiss cheese

1/2 onion, finely chopped

1 garlic clove, minced

2 tablespoons minced Italian parsley

1/4 teaspoon dried rosemary, crumbled

1/8 teaspoon pepper

Salt to taste

Gently scrape out centers of mushroom caps. Mix the scrapings with the breadcrumbs, cheese, onion, garlic, parsley, rosemary and pepper. Sprinkle a little salt on each cap and fill with the mixture. Cover and refrigerate. When ready to serve, preheat oven to broil and broil 15 minutes or until golden. Serves 4.

Boletus edulis *is one of the tastiest of the spore mushrooms. They are good-looking specimens with their rounded caps and bulbous stems. You may find dried boletes in fine markets.*

Stuffed Morels
over Asparagus Purée

A scrumptious morsel, the morel—
sheer elegance set on a pool
of asparagus purée.

Asparagus Purée, below

8 dried morels

1 cup milk for soaking
   mushrooms

2 tablespoons butter

5-6 green onions, white only,
   finely chopped

4 strips crisp, cooked bacon

1/2 cup toasted breadcrumbs

Butter a shallow baking dish. Preheat oven to 325F (160C). Slice morels in half lengthwise. Soak in milk for 20 minutes to soften.

In a large skillet, melt butter and sauté onions until soft. Crumble in bacon and add breadcrumbs. Drain and dry morels on a paper towel; fill with stuffing. Place in prepared baking dish. Bake 10 minutes, or until breadcrumb mixture is golden brown. Serve on a pool of asparagus purée. Serves 4.

Asparagus Purée
1 lb. fresh asparagus, stalks peeled

1/2 cup chicken stock

1 medium potato, boiled

Zest of 1 lime

Salt and pepper to taste

In a medium saucepan bring chicken stock to a boil, drop in asparagus and boil about 5 minutes until tender. Purée in food processor with potato until smooth. Add lime zest, salt and pepper. Keep warm until serving. Makes 1 cup.

Tender Dutch Baby
with Shaggy Mane

If the mushrooms and Parmesan are omitted, Dutch baby is a wonderful pancake to add to your breakfast repertoire. Serve with syrup, powdered sugar, fruit or jam.

4 large eggs

6 tablespoons all-purpose flour

1 tablespoon sugar

1 cup milk

1/2 lb. shaggy-mane mushrooms, coarsely chopped

3 tablespoons butter

4 tablespoons grated Parmesan cheese

1 lemon, cut in wedges

Preheat oven to 425F (220C). Beat eggs with flour, sugar and milk until smooth. Fold in mushrooms. Melt butter in a 10- or 12-inch ovenproof skillet, tilting skillet to coat. Pour in batter and set in oven slightly above center. Bake about 15 minutes until pancake puffs at edges. Quickly cut into wedges (it might deflate). Hurry to the table and pass the Parmesan cheese and lemon wedges. Serves 4.

Scarlet Polenta with Portobello

A little tomato gives a blush to the polenta and provides an extra bit of flavor. This is also a good side dish.

1-1/2 cups peeled Italian plum tomatoes

2 cups water

1 teaspoon salt

1-1/2 cups polenta or cornmeal

1/4 teaspoon pepper

1/4 cup grated Romano cheese

2 tablespoons olive oil

1 small garlic clove, finely chopped

4 mushrooms, coarsely chopped

1/4 cup black oil-cured olives, pitted

3 teaspoons olive oil

3 teaspoons unsalted butter

Purée tomatoes with their juices and strain. Place juices in large saucepan with water and bring to boil. Add salt. Slowly sprinkle in cornmeal, whisking constantly. When all cornmeal has been added, turn heat to low and cook covered, but stirring frequently for 30 minutes. Stir in pepper and cheese. Pour into an ungreased 9 x 13-inch pan, smooth with spatula, cover with plastic wrap, let cool and refrigerate for at least 2 hours or overnight.

Turn polenta onto a board and cut into 2-inch squares, or cut in pan. Cut each square in half diagonally to make 2 triangles. Set aside. Heat a large skillet over medium heat. Add 1 tablespoon oil and garlic. Cook until lightly browned. Add mushrooms and cook, stirring constantly about 10 minutes or until tender. Purée olives with 1 tablespoon oil and stir into mushrooms. Keep warm, or reheat when ready to use. Heat a large skillet and add one teaspoon each oil and butter.

Sauté polenta triangles for about 2 minutes each side, or until golden brown. Add more oil and butter for each batch. Serve hot with a heaping spoonful of mushrooms on each triangle.
Makes 24 triangles.

Warning! *As polenta begins to boil, it can bubble up and splash. Learn from another's experience and keep the lid handy while stirring the mixture.*

Timbales with Porcini, Shiitake and Buttons

You may prepare this silky-sauced first course a day ahead.

1 oz. dried porcini, soaked

1/4 lb. fresh shiitake

4 tablespoons butter

1/2 cup thinly sliced shallots

3/4 lb. button mushrooms, chopped

3 tablespoons dry white wine

1 cup chopped Italian parsley

Salt and pepper to taste

Custard

1-1/2 cups whipping cream

4 whole eggs

2 egg yolks

1/4 teaspoon ground nutmeg

Soak dried porcini in water to cover. Strain soaked porcini and chop. Chop half of shiitake, slice remainder to use as garnish. In large skillet over medium-high heat melt 2 tablespoons butter. Add shallots and sauté 3 minutes. Add button mushrooms and cook until brown and dry, stirring occasionally, about 15 minutes. Add wine, boil 1 minute. Transfer to medium bowl. In same skillet melt 1 tablespoon butter over medium-low heat. Add porcini and chopped shiitake. Cover and cook about 10 minutes until tender, stirring occasionally. Stir in parsley. Season with salt and pepper to taste. Put into bowl with button mushrooms and set aside.

Using same skillet, melt 1 tablespoon butter and sauté sliced shiitake about 5 minutes until tender. Set aside for garnish. To this point, preparation may be done a day ahead. Cover mushrooms separately and refrigerate. To continue, preheat oven to 350F (180C). Butter eight 3 to 4-inch ramekins or ovenproof custard dishes.

To prepare custard: In a large bowl combine whipping cream, eggs, egg yolks and nutmeg. Season with salt and pepper to taste and mix to creamy consistency. Place 1/3 cup mushroom mixture and 1/3 cup custard into each ramekin.

Arrange ramekins in large pan, spacing evenly. Pour hot water into pan to come halfway up sides of ramekins. Bake until set, about 40 minutes, or until knife inserted in center comes out clean. In skillet rewarm sliced shiitake over medium heat. Run sharp knife around sides of ramekins and invert timbales onto plates. Serve with sauce. Garnish with sliced shiitake. Serves 8.

Sauce
1 cup low-salt chicken broth
1/2 cup whipping cream
6 tablespoons butter
1 tablespoon minced parsley
Salt and pepper to taste

Boil broth and cream in small saucepan about 15 minutes until reduced to 1/3 cup. Gradually whisk in butter, stir in parsley, season with salt and pepper. Serve over timbales. Serves 8.

Wild Mushroom and Fontina Pizza

Oyster mushrooms and shiitake will give this pizza texture and bite. For some, this will be an entrée— or cut in thin slices as an appetizer.

2 tablespoons olive oil

3 oz. shallots, thinly sliced

1/2 lb. wild mushrooms, thinly sliced

3 fresh plum tomatoes, seeded and chopped

2 tablespoons chopped fresh thyme

2 tablespoons balsamic or red wine vinegar

Salt and pepper to taste

1 cup fontina cheese, grated

1/2 cup Cheddar cheese, grated

4 sprigs fresh thyme for garnish

Pizza crust, unbaked

Preheat oven to 500F (260C). Heat oil in large skillet over medium high. Add shallots and sauté about 4 minutes until tender. Add mushrooms and sauté about 2 minutes until tender. Add tomatoes, chopped thyme and vinegar; stir to blend. Remove from heat. Season with salt and pepper to taste. To this point, the vegetables may be prepared a day ahead. Cover and refrigerate.

Place crust on pizza pan or baking sheet. Top with 3/4 of the fontina cheese. Drain vegetables if juicy and arrange on top of cheese. Top with remaining fontina and the Cheddar. Bake about 12 minutes until cheeses melt. Cut in wedges, garnish with thyme. Serves 4.

Main Courses

Braised Duck with Sparkling Cider

Tart and sweet, a satisfying combination of flavors that charm and challenge the palate. Makes elegant dining for two.

1 duck, quartered

2 shallots, minced

1 tablespoon finely chopped fresh rosemary, or 1/2 teaspoon dried rosemary

4 sprigs fresh thyme

1 lb. turnips, peeled, sliced in 1-1/2-inch julienne

1 teaspoon sugar

2 cups sparkling cider

1 cup brown game or chicken stock

Salt and pepper to taste

1 tablespoon olive oil

1/2 lb. assorted wild mushrooms

1/2 teaspoon cider vinegar

Cut wing tips from duck below first joint. Trim flesh from wing bone. Remove excess skin and fat. Save bones for stock. Prick skin with fork. In large deep skillet sauté duck over medium heat, skin side down about 10 minutes, or until most of the fat is rendered and skin golden brown. Drain and discard fat. Turn and cook 5 more minutes. Transfer duck to plate, drain fat from skillet.

Add shallots to skillet. Cook over low heat for 2 minutes, scraping up brown bits. Add rosemary, 2 sprigs thyme and turnips. Cook 2 minutes more. Add sugar, cider, stock, salt and pepper; bring to a boil. Return duck to pan and reduce heat to low. Cover and simmer for 10 minutes. Remove breasts, continuing to cook legs for 25 minutes longer or until tender. Remove legs and turnips. Strain sauce, skim and discard fat. Set sauce aside.

In a medium pan, heat oil over high heat. Add mushrooms and cook about 5 minutes, until soft. Season with salt and pepper to taste. Add mushrooms, turnips and duck legs to sauce. Add vinegar and remaining thyme. Bring to a boil and cook uncovered over medium heat 5 to 10 minutes, until sauce is thick enough to coat a spoon. Turn legs once or twice during cooking. Add breasts and heat through. Place duck on heated platter and spoon a cup of sauce over duck. Pass remaining sauce. Serves 4.

Bread Salad with Three Mushrooms and Pesto Vinaigrette

With the combination of dried porcini, fresh shiitake and button mushrooms, this is a superb light supper. For a more substantial dinner, serve it with grilled Italian sausage.

1 (1-lb.) loaf French bread, halved lengthwise and cut into 1/2-inch slices

1 oz. dried porcini, soaked

1 whole head garlic, halved crosswise

1/4 cup plus 2 tablespoons olive oil

2 large onions, thinly sliced

1/2 teaspoon sugar

1/2 lb. button mushrooms, sliced

1/4 lb. fresh shiitake mushrooms, stemmed, sliced

Salt and pepper to taste

1 lb. tomatoes, sliced into 1/4-inch slices

1/2 cup minced fresh Italian parsley

1 cup commercial pesto vinaigrette

1 cup pitted Kalamata olives

Black pepper to taste

Butter a deep 8-cup ovenproof casserole. Arrange bread slices on large baking sheets. Let stand 2 hours at room temperature. Drain and slice soaked porcini, discarding hard stems. Reserve soaking liquid. Preheat oven to 325F (160C), toast bread about 10 minutes until slightly dry. Rub cut garlic over bread slices.

In a large skillet, heat 2 tablespoons oil over medium high, add onions, sprinkle with sugar and cook about 5 minutes, stirring frequently until onions begin to turn golden. Transfer to medium bowl. In the same skillet heat remaining 1/4 cup oil. Add button and shiitake mushrooms and cook about 3 minutes, stirring frequently. Add porcini mushrooms and stir about 1 minute until all liquid has evaporated. Season with salt and pepper to taste.

Place 1/4 toasted bread in bottom of prepared casserole, layering with 1/4 onion mixture, 1/4 mushroom mixture, 1/4 sliced tomatoes, 1/4 parsley, 1/4 pesto vinaigrette and a grind of pepper. Repeat 3 times, ending with vinaigrette. Cover with plastic wrap. To this point you may prepare this 12 hours ahead and refrigerate. To continue, let stand 3 hours at room temperature, garnish with olives and freshly ground pepper to taste. Serves 4.

Calamari Stuffed with Wild Mushrooms

*An impressive main course.
It also will star as a first course,
served one to a person.
It is not as daunting to make as it
might sound—try it.
Fresh shiitake is a good
choice of mushroom.*

1/3 cup olive oil

1/4 lb. mushrooms, sliced

1/4 cup chopped onion

1 teaspoon fresh oregano or 1/2 teaspoon dried-leaf oregano

1/2 teaspoon ground cinnamon

1/2 teaspoon freshly ground pepper

2 large garlic cloves, minced

1-1/2 cups crushed water crackers or saltines

1-1/4 cups white retsina or dry white wine

1/4 lb. feta cheese, crumbled

2 lbs. whole small calamari, or 1 lb. cleaned mantles and tentacles: there should be 8 mantles to serve 4

2 tomatoes, cored, chopped

4 fresh herb sprigs for garnish

In large skillet, heat oil. Add mushrooms, onion, oregano, cinnamon, pepper and half the garlic. Sauté about 8 minutes, stirring until onions are limp and liquid from mushrooms has evaporated. Remove from heat, stir in cracker crumbs, 1/4 cup retsina or white wine, and feta cheese until well mixed.

With fingers or small spoon, stuff mantles loosely with mushroom mixture to within 1/2 inch of opening. Do not overstuff mantles or they will ooze during cooking. Press open end of mantle together with fingers to seal loosely. Place stuffed mantles in skillet, top with tentacles, tomatoes, remaining garlic and wine and bring to a gentle boil; reduce heat to just below simmer. Cover and cook about 10 minutes, or until squid is tender when pierced. With slotted spoon, transfer mantles to serving plate, top with tomatoes, arrange tentacles at sides and keep warm. Boil pan juices over high heat, uncovered, until reduced to 1/4 cup. Pour over squid. Serves 4.

To prepare calamari or squid, clean out the mantle or squid sacs, discard cuttlebones or give them to your cat; rinse and dry the sac. Cut off tentacles and reserve for recipe. Many markets sell calamari already cleaned. Ask your butcher.

Chicken Surprise
with Agaricus Campestris

On your plate, a small golden package encases a succulent chicken breast. Lactarius or common field mushrooms are a good substitute for Agaricus campestris.

4 boneless, skinless chicken breasts

1/2 cup vermouth

Vegetable-oil spray

1/2 lb. fresh mushrooms, finely chopped

8 green onions, finely chopped

Salt and pepper to taste

8 sheets phyllo dough (1/2 package)

1/4 lb. butter, melted

Marinate chicken breasts in vermouth for 2 hours or more, turning every 30 minutes. Preheat oven to 375F (190C). Spray a baking sheet with oil. Chop mushrooms and onions and season with salt and pepper to taste.

Cut phyllo sheets in half lengthwise to make 16 sheets. Brush melted butter on 1 sheet of phyllo, cover remaining sheets with towel to keep them from drying out. Butter second sheet and lay over first. Drain one breast, place on the short end of the two sheets of phyllo, dot with butter, top with 2 tablespoons mushroom mixture and fold the corner of the dough over the chicken to make a triangle. Continue the triangle fold back and forth as you would fold a flag. As a result, each breast will be encased in 8 layers of phyllo. Repeat with remaining ingredients, using 2 sheets of phyllo per chicken breast. Bake in preheated oven for 30 to 40 minutes, or until brown and crisp. Serves 4.

How to Fold Phyllo

1.

2.

3.

4.

5.

Fish Fillets
with Chanterelles

A colorful arrangement of tender vegetables tops your favorite deep sea fillet—healthy fare for your guests.

6 (4-oz.) fish fillets such as mahi mahi, red snapper, salmon or shark

1 cup water

1/4 oz. dried chanterelles or other mushrooms

1 tablespoon oil

1 carrot, finely chopped

1 stalk celery, finely chopped

1 leek, white only, finely chopped

1 tablespoon shallots, finely chopped

4 cups fresh spinach, stems removed

1 cup water

1/2 cup vegetable stock

1/2 cup dry white wine

Salt and pepper to taste

Preheat oven to broil. Wipe fish dry and broil, allowing 5 minutes per side for each inch of thickness. Bring 1 cup water to boil in small saucepan, add dried mushrooms and boil gently for 5 minutes. Drain, chop coarsely and set aside. Keep warm.

In large skillet heat oil and sauté carrot, celery, leek and shallots for 5 minutes, or until tender.

In large pot with one cup water, steam spinach 2 to 4 minutes and drain. Set aside and keep warm. Combine vegetable stock with wine and sautéed vegetable mixture. Bring to a boil over low heat, cooking until liquid is reduced by half.

Place fillets over steamed spinach, arrange mushrooms over the spinach and top with sautéed vegetables. Pour the reduced stock over all. Add salt and pepper to taste. Serves 6.

Fish
with Black Trumpet Sauce

A pungent note of ginger spices this unusual sauce for poached fish. Though you may find black trumpets a bit ominous, they are truly delicious. You can also use morels for this recipe.

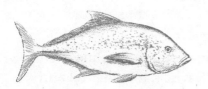

1/2 oz. dried black trumpets or other mushrooms, soaked in water to cover

Water

1 teaspoon salt

1/4 teaspoon sugar

1 tablespoon sliced green onions

1/2 teaspoon grated fresh ginger

1 tablespoon arrowroot or cornstarch

1/4 cup cold water

4 fish fillets—bass, monkfish or swordfish

Strain mushroom liquid through a fine sieve, reserve and add water to make 2 cups. Pour into a saucepan and add mushrooms, salt and sugar. Bring to a boil, lower heat and simmer 15 minutes or until liquid is reduced to 1-1/2 cups. Place mixture in a fish poacher or medium saucepan with tight-fitting lid. Add green onions and ginger; cook uncovered over medium heat until onions are wilted.

Dissolve arrowroot or cornstarch in water. Add to mushroom mixture and stir until thick. Add fish to mixture, cover and poach for 6 to 8 minutes on low until fish flakes when tested with a fork. Remove from pan, place on platter. Stir sauce, adding a little water if necessary, and pour around fish. Place some mushrooms on top for garnish. Serves 4.

Marinated Game Hens

What is more elegant than a glistening, tender game hen bathed in aromatic wild mushrooms to set before a guest? The juices are among the most delicious you will ever serve.

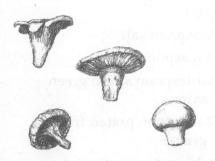

4 Cornish hens

1/2 cup olive oil

1/4 cup balsamic vinegar

2 tablespoons fresh thyme or 1-1/2 teaspoons dried-leaf thyme

Juice of 2 lemons

3 tablespoons honey

Salt and pepper to taste

4 cups assorted mushrooms such as shiitake, crimini, chanterelles, portobello and button mushrooms

Remove giblets from hens and save for another use. Rinse hens inside and out, pat dry. In a large bowl, whisk together oil and vinegar; add thyme, lemon juice, honey, salt and pepper. Place hens in a large zip-closing plastic bag, pour three-fourths of the marinade over them, seal bag and refrigerate at least 2 hours, turning frequently. Preheat oven to 350F (175C). Remove hens from marinade, place on rack in roasting pan, add 1/2 inch cold water. Roast hens 30 to 35 minutes.

While hens roast, clean mushrooms and trim stems. Cut larger mushrooms into small pieces, place in medium bowl, pour in remaining marinade and toss to coat. Pour mushrooms around hens in roasting pan and continue cooking for 10 to 15 minutes more, or until juices are clear when hens are pierced with a fork. Serves 4.

Morels and Chicken Breast on Lettuce

A melange of textures and temperatures—creamy sauce with tender chicken and mushrooms arranged over fresh young greens.

3 oz. dried morel mushrooms

1-1/2 cups Chardonnay or other dry white wine

1/4 cup shallots, finely chopped

2 cups chicken stock, page 29

1/4 cup half-and-half

1 tablespoon arrowroot or cornstarch

1 tablespoon dry white wine

1 teaspoon champagne mustard

White pepper to taste

4 whole chicken breasts, boned and skinned (8 pieces)

4 cups assorted young salad greens

1 teaspoon minced fresh tarragon

Soak mushrooms in 1/2 cup Chardonnay for 1 hour. Strain, reserve liquid. Slice morels lengthwise into 1/4-inch slices. In a small saucepan, simmer soaking liquid and shallots until reduced to 3 tablespoons. Add mushrooms and chicken stock; simmer until reduced to 1-1/4 cups. Add half-and-half. Mix arrowroot with 1 tablespoon wine and add to mixture. Add mustard. Simmer about 5 minutes until slightly thickened. Strain sauce; set mushrooms aside, keep warm. Season sauce to taste with pepper, keep warm. Lightly pound chicken breasts between sheets of waxed paper until of even thickness. Heat remaining 1 cup wine in large skillet, bring to boil. Add chicken breasts, cover, reduce heat to low and cook 3 to 5 minutes until done. Remove to heated plate, keep warm. Place salad greens on individual plates, top with chicken and sauce. Garnish with tarragon and serve at once. Serves 4.

Hungarian Lamb Stew

Roasted potatoes and sweet-and-sour red cabbage are traditionally served with this savory stew.

3 tablespoons vinegar

3 tablespoons red wine

1/2 cup cooking oil

12 peppercorns

1 bay leaf

1/2 teaspoon dried-leaf thyme

Peel of 1 lemon, sliced in strips

2 tablespoons lemon juice

1 carrot, cut in 1-inch pieces

1 onion, thinly sliced

3 sprigs parsley

3 strips bacon rind

4 to 5 lbs. leg of lamb cut into chunks (reserve the bone for soup)

3 tablespoons cooking oil, divided

1/2 lb. wild mushrooms, sliced

1/2 cup water

Sauce

2 tablespoons flour

1 cup sour cream

In a medium saucepan combine the vinegar, red wine, 1/2 cup cooking oil, peppercorns, bay leaf, thyme, lemon peel and juice, carrot, onion, parsley and bacon rind. Bring to a boil and simmer 20 minutes to make a marinade. Trim all fat from the lamb and place in large zip-closing plastic bag. Pour marinade over the lamb and refrigerate for 24 hours, turning several times a day. On cooking day, remove lamb from marinade and dry completely. Reserve marinade.

Preheat oven to 375F (190C). In a large skillet, heat 2 tablespoons oil and over high heat brown the lamb on all sides. Place lamb in an 8-cup covered casserole. In the same skillet place the remaining tablespoon oil and sauté the mushrooms over medium-high heat about 2 minutes until tender. Strain the marinade, add 1/2 cup water and pour over meat in casserole. Add the mushrooms. Cover and bake 15 minutes per pound of meat. When lamb is done, remove it and mushrooms from casserole. Skim fat from juices and discard.

To Prepare Sauce: In a medium bowl blend 2 tablespoons flour into 1 cup sour cream with whisk, gradually adding the skimmed juices. Taste for seasoning and pour the sauce back into the casserole. Return lamb to casserole, cover and return to oven. Reduce heat to 250F (120C) and bake 10 minutes more.

Arrange meat on a platter, scatter mushrooms on top and drizzle sauce over. Serves 6.

Mycogastronome: *In France—one who has enjoyed more than 100 varieties of mushrooms.*

Mushrooms
with Marinated Tofu

*A piquant vegetarian dish full of
texture; serve over rice.*

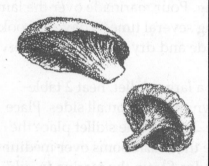

Marinade, next page

1 lb. firm tofu

1 cup mushroom stock, next
page

1 tablespoon oil

5 tablespoons butter

1 large yellow onion, finely
chopped

1/2 lb. fresh oyster
mushrooms

1/2 lb. dried shiitake, soaked

2 teaspoons garlic, minced

1 teaspoon nutritional yeast*

1/4 teaspoon dried-leaf thyme

1 tablespoon tamari

1/2 cup dry sherry or red wine

1 cup sour cream, or more
to taste

Salt and pepper to taste

Pasta or rice

Plan ahead!
The tofu in this recipe has to
marinate for 3 to 4 days.

* Nutritional yeast is available at health-food stores.

Combine marinade ingredients. Add tofu and marinate for 3 to 4 days. Prepare mushroom stock. When ready to make dish, preheat oven to 350F (180C). Remove tofu from marinade, cut into strips and bake for 20 minutes. Remove and set aside. Marinade can be saved for another use.

In large skillet, heat the oil and 1 tablespoon butter over high heat. Add onions and sauté until they begin to brown. Reduce heat to low and cook, stirring frequently, about 15 minutes, until onions begin to caramelize. As onions cook, slice both fresh and dried mushrooms and warm the mushroom stock. Mix garlic, yeast and thyme into onions. Add remaining 4 tablespoons butter and tamari. Stir and add mushrooms. Add marinated tofu and wine; simmer for 8 to 10 minutes. Add heated mushroom stock and sour cream. Cook until hot but not boiling. Taste for seasoning. Serve over pasta or rice. Serves 4.

Marinade
2 teaspoons dried oregano
2 garlic cloves, minced or pressed
1/2 cup olive oil
1/2 cup red wine vinegar
1/2 cup red wine
1/2 cup tamari sauce
1/4 teaspoon ground cloves
Salt and pepper to taste

Mushroom Stock: Soak 1/4 cup dried mushrooms in liquid of choice to cover. Remove mushrooms and save for another use. The soaking liquid becomes your mushroom stock.

Ravioli with Three Cheeses

Use your favorite pasta recipe, or purchase pasta sheets at your market for these uncommonly delicious ravioli. This recipe was created with suillus mushrooms.

Pasta dough, page 38
1/4 lb. fresh or 1/4 oz. dried mushrooms, soaked, drained, coarsely chopped
6 tablespoons ricotta cheese
3 oz. smoked mozzarella or provolone, grated
1 tablespoon whipping cream
Pepper to taste
Fresh Italian parsley, rinsed, 12 whole leaves snipped from stems

1/2 cup melted butter
1/4 cup grated Parmesan cheese

Prepare pasta dough, roll thin and cut into 24 2-inch squares. In medium bowl, place mushrooms, ricotta and mozzarella cheeses, cream and pepper. Mix well. Divide filling among 12 pasta squares, place parsley leaf on each and cover with a second pasta square. Press together edges with a dampened fingertips, then crimp edges with a fork. Ideally, parsley should be visible through the pasta. Let stand at least 10 minutes to dry slightly before cooking. In large saucepan, bring water to a boil, drop in ravioli to cook 3 minutes; drain. Serve drizzled with melted butter and sprinkled with cheese. Serves 4.

Wild Mushroom Cioppino

Celebrate this exciting mixture of fish, shellfish and mushrooms with a fine white wine.

1/3 cup olive oil

2 medium onions, chopped

1 cup finely chopped green onions, white part only

1/2 cup red bell pepper, chopped

3 garlic cloves, minced

1/4 lb. fresh wild mushrooms, chopped

1/2 cup plus 2 tablespoons chopped Italian parsley

1 (35 oz.) can Italian tomatoes, roughly chopped, with liquid

1 (16 oz.) can tomato sauce

2 cups dry red wine

1 bay leaf

1 teaspoon basil

1/2 teaspoon oregano

1/2 teaspoon salt

1/2 teaspoon freshly ground pepper

2 Dungeness crabs, cleaned and quartered, or 4 Alaskan King Crab legs cut into 4 pieces each and cracked

1 lb. firm white-fish fillets, cut into 2-inch pieces

1 lb. shrimp, shelled, tail intact

24 littleneck or cherrystone clams, well scrubbed

In a large heavy casserole heat the oil over medium heat. Add all onions, pepper and garlic; sauté about 3 minutes. Add mushrooms and sauté for 2 minutes. Add 1/2 cup parsley, tomatoes and liquid, tomato sauce, wine, bay leaf, basil, oregano, salt and pepper. Bring to a boil, reduce heat and simmer uncovered for 25 minutes. Add crabs, fish fillets and shrimp. Place clams on top in one layer; cover and simmer 10 to 12 minutes until fish is cooked and clams open. Sprinkle with remaining parsley. Serves 8.

Oscar Wild

"The only way to get rid of a temptation is to yield to it," said Oscar Wilde. It is a joy to encounter a well-cooked, beautiful meal. This version of Veal Oscar is a tribute to you, O.W.

8 (4 oz.) slices veal scallopini

1 tablespoon flour

1/2 cup mushroom duxelles, page 158, using morels

2 tablespoons oil

5 tablespoons butter, divided

4 shallots, finely chopped

8 fresh shiitake mushroom caps

2 cups dry champagne or dry white wine

1 teaspoon fresh tarragon

1/2 cup whipping cream

Salt and pepper to taste

1/2 lb. cooked asparagus

4 thin slices lemon

Chive Butter, next page

Pound veal between 2 layers of waxed paper to even thickness, taking care not to pierce the meat. Dust each slice with flour on both sides and cut in half. Spread one half with 1/2 tablespoon duxelles and place other half on top to make a sandwich. Secure with wooden picks on two sides. Repeat to make 8 sandwiches.

In a large skillet with cover, heat oil and butter over medium heat. Sauté sandwiches about 2 minutes per side. Remove to platter and keep warm. In same pan, add shallots and shiitake caps. Sauté over medium heat 2 minutes or until mushrooms are tender. Remove mushrooms and keep warm. Deglaze pan with champagne, add tarragon and cook until liquid is reduced to 1/2 cup. Stir in cream, scraping up bits from pan. Add salt and pepper to taste. Return Oscar sandwiches to pan, cover and cook 1 minute longer. To serve, top each sandwich with asparagus and a reserved mushroom cap. Garnish with a lemon slice and dot plates with chive butter. Serves 4.

Chive Butter
1/2 cup chives, coarsely chopped
3 tablespoons butter

Pulse chives and butter in food processor until smooth.

As Rita Tells It. . .

Afloat in Sumatra

It was one of those tropical nights on the Ala River in Sumatra. We had pitched our tents on the river bank, and were bemoaning the fact that in all this jungle we had found no fungi. Sometime later, when darkness was upon us and every noise had subsided, there came a rousing shout: "Mushrooms!" It was like the call of a bugle, and all ten of us ran to stand barefoot around a tree stump, staring at a cluster of opalescent, luminescent mushrooms that our friend had discovered on a midnight excursion.

Puffballs, Pasta and Shrimp

A handsome dish perfumed with spices.

1/3 cup olive oil

2 lbs. shrimp, in shells

2 tablespoons cognac

1 carrot, shredded

1 onion, finely chopped

10 cherry tomatoes, quartered

1/4 teaspoon saffron

1/4 teaspoon cayenne pepper

1/4 teaspoon salt

2 cups dry white wine

1 cup sour cream

3/4 cup butter

2 garlic cloves, finely chopped

1 lb. fresh puffballs, chopped

1 lb. fettucine, cooked al dente

Chopped parsley

Puffball Lycoperdon perlatum *comes in sizes from small button to the herculean size of a coffee table. Imagine encountering the latter! A fungophilean dream!*

Heat 1/3 cup oil in a large covered skillet over medium heat, add shrimp in shells and sauté about 1 minute until shrimp turn pink. Pour in the cognac and ignite. Shake pan back and forth until flames die out. With slotted spoon, transfer shrimp to a medium bowl. Peel shrimp and place shells in the skillet. Add carrot, onion, tomatoes, saffron, cayenne pepper, salt and 1-1/2 cups wine. Cover and simmer 15 minutes, stirring occasionally. Add sour cream and remaining wine. Simmer uncovered 10 minutes. Strain mixture into a medium bowl, pressing to extract as much liquid as possible. Discard solids.

In the same skillet melt 1/2 cup (1 stick) butter over low heat, add garlic and mushrooms. Cook covered for 20 minutes, stirring occasionally. Remove from heat. To assemble, heat reserved liquid and peeled shrimp, adding remaining butter and mushrooms. Heat through. Place hot pasta on large heated platter and toss with mushrooms, shrimp and sauce. Sprinkle with chopped parsley. Serves 4.

Salmon Fillets with Wild Mushroom Ragout

For best flavor and character use only wild mushrooms in the ragout. A mix of varieties is especially good in this recipe.

3 tablespoons butter

5 shallots, minced

1-1/4 lbs. mixed mushrooms, such as oyster, chanterelle or morel

3/4 cup bottled clam juice

3/4 cup dry white wine

3 tablespoons whipping cream

2 teaspoons chopped fresh tarragon or 1/2 teaspoon dried-leaf tarragon

Salt and pepper to taste

6 salmon fillets

2 tablespoons melted butter

2 tablespoons lemon juice

Salt and pepper to taste

Fresh tarragon sprigs for garnish

In a large skillet melt 3 tablespoons butter, add shallots and sauté 2 minutes. Increase heat to medium high, add mushrooms and sauté about 8 minutes, until beginning to brown. Add clam juice and wine. Boil 20 minutes until liquid has almost evaporated. Cover and chill. May be prepared to this point 6 hours ahead.

To continue, preheat broiler. Warm mushroom mixture, add cream, bring to a simmer and cook about 1 minute until thickened, stirring constantly. Mix in chopped tarragon and season with salt and pepper. Keep warm. Arrange salmon skin-side down on broiler pan. Brush with mixture of melted butter and lemon juice. Sprinkle with salt and pepper. Broil without turning 10 minutes per inch of thickness until cooked through. Remove skin before serving. Transfer to plates, spoon on mushrooms and garnish with tarragon sprigs. Serves 6.

Scallops Chardonnay
with Duxelles

Serve this delicate offering over mini puff pastries as a first course, or use larger puff pastries and serve as an entrée with peas and salad.

1 cup whipping cream

1/3 cup Chardonnay or dry white wine

2 tablespoons mushroom duxelles, page 158

2 tablespoons flour

2 tablespoons melted butter

Salt and pepper to taste

1 lb. scallops, rinsed and dried

4 baked puff pastries

Pour water into the bottom of a double boiler, not allowing it to touch bottom of upper pan. Heat water to a simmer. In the upper boiler place the cream, wine and duxelles and heat, do not boil. In a medium skillet over medium heat, make a roux by mixing the flour with butter, stirring constantly until smooth and golden. Whisk in mushroom mixture and stir constantly until it thickens. Transfer back to double boiler and add scallops to sauce. The scallops will cook in the hot sauce without becoming overdone. Serve over puff pastry cut into shapes of your choice. Serves 4.

Stir-fry with Russula and Tofu

A quick and satisfying meal is yours with this medley of russula mushrooms and vegetables. Serve it over rice or noodles.

1/2 oz. dried russula mushrooms

2 cups Chardonnay or other dry white wine

2 tablespoons peanut oil

1 cup broccoli florets

2 garlic cloves, chopped

1 cup firm tofu cut into 1/2-inch cubes

Soak mushrooms in Chardonnay for 1 hour, drain and reserve liquid. Chop mushrooms and set aside. In large skillet or wok, heat oil to smoking, add broccoli and stir-fry 1 minute. Add mushrooms and garlic, cook 1 minute more. Add mushroom soaking liquid and tofu; continue stirring 1 to 2 minutes until tofu is lightly browned and liquid is reduced by half. Serves 4.

Russula decolorans *is a rusty-red-and-yellow mushroom, a colorful fellow common to the southern Rockies.* Lactarius *is another of the russula family. Still another,* Piparatus, *yields a milk that tastes like Tabasco® sauce!*

Game Hens
with Pasta

Lingonberries or cranberries make a lovely accompaniment to these honey and-mustard-coated little birds. Use boletes if you can.

The sauce in this recipe is wonderful with any game.

1 oz. dried mushrooms

2 cups hot water

3 tablespoons butter

1/2 cup onions, finely chopped

3 tablespoons flour

1 cup meat stock, preferably from game

1/2 cup dry red wine

1/2 teaspoon each allspice, paprika and sugar

1 small dill pickle, minced

Salt and pepper to taste

4 Cornish hens or squabs

1/2 cup honey

1 tablespoon Dijon mustard

4 cups cooked pasta

In a saucepan soak mushrooms in 2 cups hot water for 2 hours, then bring to a boil. Reduce heat; simmer 30 minutes. Drain and set aside, reserving liquid.

In a large skillet, prepare a roux: melt butter, sauté onion until transparent. Add flour, stirring constantly. A little at a time, pour in stock, wine and liquid from mushrooms. Stir until mixture is smooth. Simmer 15 minutes. Add allspice, paprika, sugar, dill pickle, salt and pepper. Taste for seasoning. Set aside.

Preheat oven to broil. Cut Cornish hens or squabs in half, brush with mixture of honey and mustard and broil for 20 to 25 minutes, turning once. Arrange on platter over pasta with sauce. Serves 4.

Strudel
with Chanterelles

Rita has prepared this recipe at the Fungophile conference in Telluride, Colorado for the last seven years. It is an awesome sight to see her stretch a handful of dough the length and width of a table.

Strudel Dough

2 cups unbleached flour

1 small egg, lightly beaten

2 teaspoons vinegar

1/2 cup warm water

2 tablespoons lard or oil

1 teaspoon oil

1 cup melted butter

Preheat oven to 375F (190C). Bring all ingredients to room temperature. Place flour in a medium bowl, make a well in center and add egg. Stir in vinegar, water and 2 tablespoons lard or oil. Knead dough about 10 minutes until smooth and satiny. Brush top with 1 teaspoon oil, cover with bowl and let dough rest 30 minutes.

Spread tablecloth on a table or large smooth surface. Sprinkle cloth with flour. Place dough in center. Beat with rolling pin to flatten a bit, then begin rolling out from the center in all directions. When you have rolled it as thin as possible, slip fingers under edge of dough, lifting it with the backs of your hands to release it from the cloth. Brush lightly with melted butter. Again slip hands under dough. From the center, with backs of hands and fingertips, stretch and manipulate the dough until you achieve a see-through consistency. The stretched dough should be approximately 3 feet square.

Strudel Filling

1 tablespoon oil
2 tablespoons butter
1 medium onion, minced
2 lbs. fresh wild mushrooms, coarsely chopped
3/4 tablespoon whipping cream
Zest of 1 lemon
1 tablespoon chopped Italian parsley
Salt and pepper to taste

1/4 lb. melted butter
1 egg yolk, well beaten

In a large skillet sauté onion in oil and butter. Add mushrooms, cream and lemon zest and cook over high heat until liquid is absorbed. Add parsley, salt and pepper.

Filling and Rolling the Strudel: In preparation for filling and rolling up the strudel, trim away rough edges of the dough with scissors. Brush the entire surface with melted butter, place filling at one end and gently roll up, using the cloth to lift and roll. Beginning at the side of the table nearest you, lift and roll the strudel toward the opposite side of the table. When you have rolled the entire strudel, brush it with beaten egg yolk. Spray a large baking pan with cooking spray, fold the strudel into a horseshoe shape to fit it on the sheet. Bake 40 to 50 minutes, or until lightly browned. Cool slightly and slice. Makes about 20 slices.

Instead of making the strudel dough, you may substitute 1 (17-1/4 oz.) package frozen phyllo dough, thawed. Brush each phyllo leaf with melted butter.

Vegetarian Shiitake Stir-fry

Over noodles or rice, and topped with sesame seeds, this is a new twist for stir-fry enthusiasts. The beefy texture of the shiitake will satisfy meat lovers as well as those of a vegetarian persuasion.

4 oz. firm tofu cut into 3/4-inch cubes

2 tablespoons soy sauce

1 (1-oz.) pkg. dried shiitake mushrooms, soaked in 2 cups water

2 to 3 tablespoons peanut or olive oil

1 lb. broccoli flowers

1 garlic clove, minced

2 teaspoons fresh ginger, shredded

1 red onion, sliced in thin wedges

1/4 oz. fresh enoki mushrooms or a 4-oz. jar straw mushrooms*

3 tablespoons dry sherry

1 teaspoon cornstarch

1/4 teaspoon sugar

1/2 teaspoon mashed fermented black beans*

1 teaspoon sesame seeds, toasted

Black pepper to taste

4 sprigs cilantro for garnish

* Fermented beans may be found in packages in Asian markets. They add a dense, mysterious flavor that tickles the taste buds. Straw mushrooms are also found in Asian markets or the Asian section of specialty markets.

In a small bowl, toss tofu with soy sauce. Set aside. Drain mushrooms into another small bowl, adding strained soaking liquid to tofu. Slice mushrooms. In a wok or large skillet, heat oil over high heat to smoking. Using slotted spoon, remove tofu from marinade. Reserve marinade. Add tofu to wok, stir-fry 1 minute or until browned. Remove and set aside. Add broccoli, garlic and ginger to wok and stir-fry 2 minutes. Add onion, shiitake and enoki mushrooms and stir-fry 1 minute. Pour in tofu marinade, bring to a boil and simmer 2 minutes or until broccoli is tender crisp. Stir in tofu. Blend sherry, cornstarch and sugar, pour into wok and cook, stirring until thickened. Add fermented beans and toasted sesame seeds. Season with a grind of pepper. Garnish with cilantro. Serves 4.

A Wild Tart

*Use leccinum mushrooms if you come
across them. Otherwise, porcini makes
this a lovely presentation for lunch,
a light supper or, in mini portions,
a choice hors d'oeuvre.*

1 (9-inch) frozen pie crust
3/4 oz. dried mushrooms
2 cups water or dry red wine
2 tablespoons unsalted butter
1/2 cup shallots
2-1/2 teaspoons minced garlic
2 tablespoons cognac
3/4 lb. fresh mushrooms

Salt and pepper to taste
3 large eggs
1-1/4 cups half-and-half
1/2 teaspoon dried-leaf basil
1/4 teaspoon dried-leaf thyme
2 cups grated Swiss cheese
Italian parsley for garnish

Preheat oven to 375F (190C). Line pie crust with foil, fill with pie
weights or dried beans. Bake 10 minutes, remove weights and foil
and bake about 15 minutes until crust begins to color, piercing with
fork if it puffs. Set aside to cool. Maintain oven temperature.

Soak dried mushrooms in water or wine. Drain and chop
soaked mushrooms, reserve liquid. In large skillet, melt butter,
sauté shallots and garlic 1 minute on high. Add cognac and
reserved soaking liquid. Chop fresh mushrooms and add to skillet,
sauté about 3 minutes until mushrooms release their liquids and
liquids evaporate. Add drained soaked mushrooms and cook 5
minutes more. Season with salt and pepper to taste. In medium
bowl, whisk eggs, half-and-half, basil and thyme until blended.
Combine with mushroom mixture. Add salt and pepper to taste.
Sprinkle half of grated cheese on partially baked crust. Top with
mushroom mixture and remaining cheese. Bake in preheated oven
about 30 minutes until center is set. Transfer to rack, cool and garnish with parsley. Serves 4.

Sherried Leek, Squash and Flammulina Mushroom Stew

A flammulina, a little flame—gather your guests, and perform this simple mushroom show with flair!

2 tablespoons olive oil

3 cups fresh mushrooms

3 cups julienne leeks

1-1/2 cups julienne zucchini

1-1/2 cups julienne yellow squash

4 garlic cloves, finely chopped

3/4 cup dry sherry or cognac

1 cup chicken stock, page 29

2 cups green onions, thinly sliced on the bias

3 cups chopped canned tomatoes, drained

Salt and pepper to taste

In a large skillet over medium high, heat the oil. Add the mushrooms, leeks, zucchini, yellow squash and garlic; sauté for 2 minutes. Pour in the sherry and carefully set aflame. When flame subsides, add the chicken stock. Let simmer about 3 minutes. Add green onions and tomatoes, cook 1 more minute. Add salt and pepper to taste. Serves 4.

Flammulinas grow on the trunks of deciduous trees. A sister variety (the enoki) sold in markets is a cultivated variety.

Tuna
with Mushroom Medley

A blanket of succulent mushrooms gives tuna steaks a fashionable new look, and new gustatory delight.

4 tablespoons olive oil

4 (6 oz.) slices fresh tuna

4 tablespoons butter

1 lb. mixed mushrooms, sliced

1 garlic clove, finely chopped

1/4 teaspoon dried oregano leaves

1/4 teaspoon dried rosemary, crumbled

1 tablespoon water

Salt and pepper to taste

Parsley sprigs for garnish

Heat olive oil in a large skillet. Sprinkle tuna steaks with salt and pepper to taste and fry for 5 minutes on each side. Remove to platter and keep warm. In same skillet, melt butter and add mushrooms, garlic, oregano and rosemary. Stir and cook for 10 minutes. Add 1 tablespoon water to juices in pan. Add salt and pepper. Pour skillet mixture over tuna steaks and garnish with parsley sprigs. Serves 4.

Pork Chops
with Mushrooms

This entrée is a succulent marinated meat teamed with mushrooms which hold their shape. Use hedgehogs, Lactarius delicioso or Armillaria mellea.

4 (6-oz.) lean, bone-in pork
  chops

Marinade

2 cups dry white wine

2 bay leaves

1 sprig fresh rosemary

1 whole garlic clove

Zest of 1 orange

1/2 cup all-purpose flour

1/4 cup olive oil

1 clove garlic, finely chopped

1 small green chile pepper

1 tablespoon capers

1 lb. mushrooms

6 tablespoons chicken stock,
  page 29

Place pork chops in a baking dish. Combine marinade ingredients and pour over pork chops. Cover and refrigerate 24 hours. Remove chops and pat dry, dust with flour. In a large saucepan heat oil; cook chops over medium heat until brown on both sides. Remove chops and set aside. To the same pan add chopped garlic, chile, capers and the mushrooms. Sauté about 2 minutes. Reduce heat to low. Add marinade and stock and return pork chops to pan. Cover and cook over low heat for 35 minutes. Serves 4.

Beef with Chanterelles and Shiitake

A hearty, satisfying dish for your friends.

1/4 cup olive oil

1 lb. beef fillet

Salt and pepper to taste

8 oz. mixed mushrooms, sliced into bite-size pieces

1 garlic clove, finely chopped

1 tablespoon parsley, finely chopped

1 cup dry red wine

In a large heavy skillet heat 2 tablespoons oil over medium-high heat and add beef, turning to seal all sides. Reduce heat to low, season meat with salt and pepper and cook 10 minutes, turning occasionally, making sure beef remains pink inside. Remove from pan; cover and keep warm. Add remaining 2 tablespoons oil to same skillet and stir-fry mushrooms 4 minutes. Add garlic and parsley and continue cooking 2 minutes until mushrooms are tender. Add the wine. When wine has evaporated, taste for seasoning. Arrange meat on serving platter and cover with mushrooms. Serves 4.

Side Dishes

Black Beans and Puffballs

Give new life to black beans with the addition of mushrooms. Use this with any meat, or for your next Mexican meal.

Olive-oil cooking spray

2 shallots, coarsely chopped

2 garlic cloves, finely chopped

3/4 lb. puffballs, coarsely chopped

1 tablespoon tamari sauce

1/2 teaspoon dry mustard powder

1 cup chicken broth

1 teaspoon fermented black beans, mashed*

2 cans black beans, rinsed and drained

1 teaspoon cornmeal

2 tablespoons ground cumin

Salt and pepper to taste

Spray a large skillet with olive-oil spray, and sauté shallots and garlic over medium-high heat until browned. Add mushrooms and tamari sauce and cook 3 minutes. Add dry mustard powder, chicken broth, fermented beans, drained black beans, cornmeal, cumin, salt and pepper. Stir to combine. Reduce heat to low and simmer until liquid has reduced so that beans are moist but not soupy. Serves 4.

* Fermented beans may be found in packages in Asian markets. They add a dense, mysterious flavor that tickles the taste buds.

Black Trumpet Soufflé

Recently I was amazed to find fresh black trumpets at a market in Tucson, and immediately grabbed them up for one of my classes. My students were delighted.

1 (1/4 oz.) pkg dried black trumpets or other mushrooms
1 cup warm water
1/4 cup butter
1/2 cup all-purpose flour
1-1/4 cups milk
3/4 cup grated Swiss cheese
Salt and pepper to taste
3 eggs, separated
4 sprigs parsley for garnish

Preheat oven to 425F (220C). Butter a deep 4-cup soufflé dish. Soak black trumpets in 1 cup warm water for 20 minutes, rinse and strain. In medium saucepan, melt butter, add mushrooms and sauté 5 minutes or until tender. If mushrooms exude a lot of liquid, remove them with a slotted spoon and boil liquid over high heat until reduced by half, then return mushrooms to pan. Add flour and cook, stirring constantly for 2 minutes. Remove from heat, gradually stir in milk. Return to heat and cook, stirring until smooth and very thick. Stir in cheese. Remove from heat again and season with salt and pepper. Cool slightly, then beat in egg yolks one at a time. In a medium bowl whisk egg whites until stiff. Carefully fold into mushroom mixture. Pour into prepared soufflé dish, place in oven on center rack and immediately reduce heat to 350F (175C). Bake 40 to 45 minutes or until risen, browned and firm on top. Garnish with parsley and serve at once. Serves 4.

Russian Chanterelle Casserole

*From Russia with love.
When the cold northern winds
are howling, serve this
mushroom casserole.*

1 lb. eggplant

2 cups water

3/4 lb. chanterelles or other
  mushrooms

3-1/2 tablespoons butter

1/4 teaspoon salt

Juice of 1 lemon

1-1/2 tablespoons flour

1/2 cup milk

1/4 cup whipping cream

Salt and pepper to taste

1/2 teaspoon nutmeg

1 egg, lightly beaten

2 tablespoons breadcrumbs

2 tablespoons grated
  Parmesan cheese

Preheat oven to 325F (160C). Butter a 6-cup ovenproof casserole.
Peel eggplant and cut into 1-inch cubes. In a 3-quart saucepan
bring 2 cups water to boil; add the eggplant, cook 5 minutes and
drain. Slice the mushrooms. There should be about 3 cups. In a
large skillet melt 1 tablespoon butter and add mushrooms. Sprinkle
with salt and 1 teaspoon lemon juice. Cook, stirring, until mushrooms are wilted and have released their juices. Continue cooking
until the liquid has evaporated. Remove from pan and set aside.

In the same skillet, melt 1-1/2 tablespoons butter. Whisk in flour. Stir in milk and cream. When smooth, add salt and pepper to taste, nutmeg and remaining lemon juice. Stir in mushrooms, egg-plant and beaten egg. Spoon mixture into prepared casserole and sprinkle with crumbs and Parmesan cheese. Dot with remaining tablespoon butter. Bake in preheated oven 30 to 40 minutes, then increase oven heat to broil and quickly brown the top. Serves 4.

As Rita Tells It. . .
Out of Africa

Coming down from halfway up Kilimanjaro, our group met with rain, our stomachs already growling like thunder. There they stood like a miracle! *Termitomyces* mushrooms! With their long stems and wide caps, they looked like small umbrellas as they stood growing on terrestrial termite mounds of monumental size—some tall as a house!

Our guide Gary, overjoyed as I was, told us that these mush-rooms bring some of the highest prices of any edible mushrooms. Growing in some mysterious symbiosis with the termites, they eventually destroy the mound with their long underground stems. Then the termites have to vacate and build a new mound and the process begins again.

Later that evening in a candlelit kitchen I melted some clarified butter over a kerosene stove, fried up these *dampshades* and served them with bamboo picks at a well-earned happy hour.

Chanterelle
and Cheese Pancakes

Delicate mini pancakes should be made with the smallest chanterelles you can find. Serve a few as golden-brown accompaniment to meat dishes, or as an hors d'oeuvre with herbed butter.

1/2 cup milk

1-1/4 cups dry, crustless, 1/2-inch white-bread cubes

4 tablespoons clarified butter, next page

1/2 cup coarsely chopped fresh chanterelle mushrooms

1 egg, lightly beaten

1-3/4 oz. (1/2 cup) shredded Cantal or Monterey Jack

Salt and white pepper to taste

Pour milk over bread in a medium bowl. Soak 3 minutes. Strain liquid through a fine sieve, pressing gently with the back of a spoon. Discard milk. You should have 1/3 cup bread. Return bread to bowl. Brush a small non-stick skillet with clarified butter, add mushrooms and cook over medium heat 2 to 3 minutes, stirring occasionally, until liquid has almost evaporated.

Stir beaten egg into soaked bread with a fork until well blended. Mix in cheese. Add chanterelles. Season with salt and white pepper to taste. To this point, batter may be prepared 3 hours ahead. Cover and keep at room temperature.

When ready to proceed, preheat oven to low heat. Heat a large skillet over medium low, brush lightly with clarified butter. Ladle batter into skillet by tablespoonfuls. Cook 5 minutes until brown, turn and cook other side until brown and cooked through. Transfer pancakes to a baking sheet and keep warm in oven. Repeat with remaining batter, brushing skillet with clarified butter as needed. Serve immediately. Makes 12 (2-inch) pancakes.

To Prepare Clarified Butter: In a small saucepan melt butter, skim off foam and pour clear yellow liquid into a small container, leaving milky residue at the bottom. The clear liquid is non-sticking clarified butter.

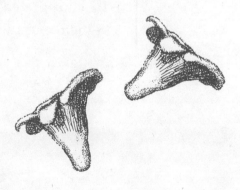

Asian-style Egg Rolls

Looks like canneloni, but actually is an Asian medley of mushrooms and pungent seasonings that stimulate the palate.

2 oz. dried shiitake
  mushrooms

7 tablespoons butter

1-1/2 cups button
  mushrooms, thinly sliced

1 garlic clove, minced

3 tablespoons white wine
  vinegar

1-1/2 teaspoons soy sauce

2/3 cup dry sherry

4-1/2 teaspoons minced fresh
  ginger

1 teaspoon dry mustard

1-3/4 teaspoons ground
  coriander

1/4 cup all-purpose flour

1-3/4 cups chicken stock,
  page 29

3/4 cup milk

1-1/2 cups grated Swiss cheese

8 (6-inch) egg-roll wrappers

Soak dried mushrooms in 2 cups water or wine. Preheat oven to 425F (220C). Spray 9 x 13-inch baking dish with oil. Drain soaked mushrooms and slice. Remove and discard stems. In large skillet melt 4 tablespoons butter over medium heat. Add sliced button mushrooms and garlic and cook about 25 minutes, stirring often until liquid has evaporated. Add vinegar, soy sauce, 1/3 cup sherry, 3 teaspoons ginger, 3/4 teaspoon dry mustard and 1 teaspoon coriander. Cook, stirring, until liquid evaporates. Set aside.

In another large skillet over medium heat, melt 3 tablespoons butter and blend in flour, remaining ginger, dry mustard and coriander. Cook, stirring until bubbly. Remove from heat and whisk in stock and milk. Return to heat, bring to rapid boil. Remove and add 1 cup cheese and remaining sherry. Stir 1 cup sauce into mushrooms. Lay egg-roll wrappers flat, spread 1 tablespoon filling along edge of each and roll up. Seal by running dampened finger along edges. Arrange seam-side down in baking dish. Sprinkle with remaining cheese. You may cover and refrigerate overnight at this time, or proceed. Bake about 20 minutes until bubbles appear. Serves 4.

Creamed Chanterelles and Oysters

A warm and satiny side dish blanketed with crunchy crumbs is beautiful served in individual scallop shells—just as nice when baked in a casserole.

1 oz. dried mushrooms

1 cup water

3 tablespoons butter

1 cup fresh breadcrumbs

Salt to taste

White pepper to taste

3 tablespoons chopped shallots

2 tablespoons water

1 tablespoon plus 1 teaspoon all purpose flour

Whipping cream

1 pt. shucked oysters, liquor reserved

1-1/4 tablespoons Madeira

1/4 teaspoon mace

2 tablespoons chopped fresh Italian parsley

Soak mushrooms in water, drain and chop. Preheat oven to 350F (175C). In a large skillet, melt 1 tablespoon butter. Add bread-crumbs, stir until crisp and brown. Transfer to small bowl and set aside. Add 1 tablespoon butter to skillet, add mushrooms, cook over medium heat 2 to 3 minutes, stirring occasionally. Season with salt and white pepper to taste. Cook about 4 minutes more until cooked through, but not browned. Set aside.

Melt remaining tablespoon butter in a medium saucepan. Add shallots and water, cook until soft but not browned. Add flour, stir about 1 minute, thinning with cream or oyster liquid a tablespoon at a time, if necessary. To this point, you may prepare this recipe 4 hours ahead.

Reheat sauce in skillet before proceeding. Drain oysters, cut them in half or thirds with sharp scissors and add to skillet. Cook over medium heat about 1 minute until their edges begin to curl. Stir mushrooms, oysters, Madeira and mace into sauce. Heat until warm. Do not boil. Spoon into scallop shells, place on baking sheet and sprinkle with breadcrumbs. Bake about 7 minutes until piping hot. Garnish with parsley. Serves 4.

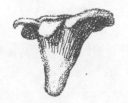  

Polish Hunters' Potatoes

Here is my version of an old Polish dish that was originated by hunters during the bear and boar season. This lasted them several days, improving as flavors blended.

8 slices bacon, cut in half

4 medium potatoes, sliced

6 carrots, sliced

1 lb. wild mushrooms, sliced

2 medium onions, thinly sliced

1 lb. Polish sausage links, sliced

1 large green or red cabbage, sliced

Salt to taste

Oil a large casserole. Preheat oven to 400F (200C). Cover bottom of casserole with bacon slices, then make 4 layers, each containing potatoes, carrots, mushrooms, onions, sausage and cabbage. Lightly salt each layer. End with cabbage. Cover and bake 2 hours, or until potatoes are tender. Let stand until cool and refrigerate until needed; reheat and serve. Serves 6.

This is a hearty and filling camping dish you may cook over a fire. At home, use the oven. Make it a day or so ahead so the flavors ripen.

Roasted Mushrooms with Pine Nuts

This classic Sicilian recipe is served with Italian flat bread such as Boboli® or foccacia. Agaricus campestris is my favorite for this recipe.

2 tablespoons olive oil

24 to 30 large mushrooms

1 lemon, halved

4 large garlic cloves, minced

2/3 cup shelled pine nuts

Salt and pepper to taste

1/2 teaspoon dried red-pepper flakes

5 tablespoons olive oil

Preheat oven to 400F (200C). Use 2 tablespoons oil to grease an 11 x 7-inch baking dish. Brush mushrooms to clean. Rub all over with lemon. Remove stems, slice, place in bowl and set aside. Place mushroom caps in dish stem side up. They should fit snugly. Sprinkle sliced stems over the caps with minced garlic, pine nuts, salt and pepper. Sprinkle red pepper flakes evenly on top. Drizzle on oil. Bake in top part of oven for 15 to 20 minutes, or until pine nuts begin to brown. Serve hot or at room temperature. Serves 4.

Mushroom Gratin

Creamy Gruyère cheese combines with crunchy breadcrumbs for a mouth-watering topping. Buttery oyster mushrooms are a good choice, as well.

2 tablespoons butter

2 finely sliced shallots

1 lb. mixed fresh wild mushrooms

1/4 cup Madeira wine

1/8 cup dry sherry

1 cup chicken stock, page 29

1/2 cup whipping cream

1/4 cup finely chopped Italian parsley

1/2 cup grated Gruyère cheese

1/2 cup breadcrumbs

Butter an ovenproof platter or shallow baking dish. In a large skillet over medium-high heat melt butter and sauté shallots and mushrooms about 5 minutes until tender. Remove from pan and set aside. Reduce heat to medium. In same skillet heat Madeira and sherry and deglaze pan, scraping up loose bits and pieces. Add chicken stock, bring to a boil and reduce to about 1/2 cup. Add cream and cook 5 to 8 minutes, stirring until sauce coats a wooden spoon. Mix in mushrooms and pour onto prepared platter or baking dish.

Preheat broiler. Mix chopped parsley, Gruyère cheese and breadcrumbs. Spread evenly over mushrooms and place under broiler about 3 minutes until breadcrumbs have browned. Serves 3.

Mushroom Sauté with Tomatoes

This robust and colorful companion to a meat course will satisfy a hearty appetite.

2 tablespoons olive oil

3 large portobello mush-
rooms, coarsely chopped

1 tablespoon capers

2 chopped fresh tomatoes

1/4 teaspoon dried red-
pepper flakes, or to taste

2 teaspoons cornstarch

1/4 cup cold water

Salt and pepper to taste

In large skillet heat olive oil and sauté mushrooms about 5 minutes until tender. Add capers, tomatoes and pepper flakes. Dissolve cornstarch in water and stir into mushroom mixture. Stir constantly to thicken slightly. Add salt and pepper to taste. Cook 1 minute. Serves 4.

Asian Pasta
with Wood Ear

This salad is a lovely foil for your prettiest Asian garnishes, like radish roses or carrot flowers. Wood ears really do expand to several times their size, so use a large pan for boiling.

1 wood ear soaked in water to cover

1 tablespoon sesame oil

3 tablespoons sesame seeds

Dressing

1/2 cup mushroom liquid

1/2 cup soy sauce

1/4 cup chicken stock, page 29

1 tablespoon sugar

1/2 lb. pasta cooked, drained

1/4 cup sesame oil

6 green onions cut into fine strips

Soak mushrooms; drain. In large saucepan cover soaked mushrooms with boiling water and boil gently for 10 minutes. Drain and reserve 1/2 cup liquid. Cut mushrooms in 1/4-inch strips and set aside. In small skillet heat 1 tablespoon sesame oil and toast sesame seeds until golden. Set aside.

In a small bowl combine 1/2 cup mushroom liquid, soy sauce, chicken stock and sugar and mix well.

In a large bowl toss dressing with mushroom slices and pasta. Drizzle 1/4 cup sesame oil over the pasta, sprinkle with toasted sesame seeds and garnish with green onion strips. Serves 4.

Auricularia polytricha—*wood ears are jelly fungi that become hard and firm when dry. Wood ear mushrooms were first cultivated in China.*

Mushrooms in Garlic Butter over Pasta

A pungent garlic-and-onion sauce tops linguine. And imagine discovering that a bit of this delicious sauce is also wonderful over mashed potatoes.

1 tablespoon butter

1 tablespoon oil

4 garlic cloves, minced

3 finely chopped green onions

1 lb. oyster mushrooms, coarsely chopped

Salt and pepper to taste

Juice of half a lemon

1/2 lb. linguine, cooked, drained

Heat butter and oil in large skillet with cover over medium heat. Add garlic and onions. Stir and cook about 3 minutes until tender. Mix in mushrooms, cover and cook for 5 minutes. Stir and add salt and pepper to taste. Sprinkle with lemon juice and pour over pasta. Serves 4.

Polenta with Fontina Cheese and Oyster Mushrooms

Those who appreciate good food have learned to love polenta, the Italian cornmeal mush. It is a simple, nutritious substitute for rice, potatoes or pasta.

3 cups water

1 tablespoon olive oil

1/2 teaspoon salt

1 cup yellow cornmeal

5 tablespoons unsalted butter, cut into pieces

Pepper to taste

1/2 cup freshly grated Parmesan cheese

5 oz. fontina cheese, sliced thin

Oyster Mushroom Sauce, next page

2 tablespoons chopped fresh Italian parsley for garnish

Oil a 9-inch-square baking dish. In a medium saucepan bring water, olive oil and salt to boil. Stirring constantly, add cornmeal in thin stream. Reduce heat to low; cover and cook about 40 minutes, stirring frequently. Use pot cover as a shield against spattering when you remove it to stir. Polenta is done when it begins to leave the sides of the pan. Add pieces of butter, stir until melted.

Immediately spread polenta in prepared dish, smooth top, cool completely. May be prepared a day ahead to this point. Cover with plastic wrap and refrigerate. Bring to room temperature before proceeding.

Preheat oven to 350F (175C). Butter large baking sheet. Turn polenta out onto a board. Sprinkle on pepper and Parmesan cheese, and top with slices of fontina. Cut into 2-1/2-inch pieces. Makes 24 pieces. Transfer polenta to prepared baking sheet, spacing evenly. Bake about 20 minutes until cheese melts and polenta is heated through. Meanwhile, prepare Oyster Mushroom Sauce.

To serve, place baked polenta on plates, surround with sauce and top with parsley. Serves 6.

Oyster Mushroom Sauce

3 tablespoons olive oil

3 garlic cloves, sliced thin

3/4 lb. fresh oyster mushrooms,
   trimmed and halved

Salt to taste

Heat 3 tablespoons oil in large skillet over medium-high heat. Add sliced garlic and sauté 1 minute. Add mushrooms and sauté about 5 minutes until golden. Season with salt to taste.

Warning! *Be careful when removing cover while polenta is cooking. It spatters and can give a fierce burn. Use the pot cover as a shield against spattering.*

Porcini Linguine

*Begin preparing this recipe
one day ahead to allow
yogurt cheese time to drain.*

1/2 oz. dried porcini
   mushrooms, soaked
   and chopped

2-1/2 cups water

1 large carrot, cut in 1/4-inch
   julienne sticks

1 tablespoon oil

5 medium shallots, finely
   chopped

3 large garlic cloves, minced

1 lb. fresh oyster mushrooms,
   coarsely chopped

1 lb. fresh shiitake
   mushrooms, coarsely
   chopped

1/2 cup dry white wine

1-1/2 teaspoons finely
   chopped fresh thyme

1 cup yogurt cheese, next page

Salt and pepper to taste

3/4 lb. linguine, cooked,
   drained

1/4 cup finely chopped Italian
   parsley or chervil

1/4 cup grated Parmesan
   cheese

Soak dried mushrooms in 2 cups water. Drain and reserve soaking liquid. Chop mushrooms.

In a small saucepan heat 1/2 cup water and simmer carrots until tender. Drain and set aside. In a large skillet heat oil and sauté shallots and garlic until tender. Add all mushrooms and cook about 3 minutes until tender. Increase heat to high, add wine and boil for 2 minutes. Add reserved soaking liquid, carrot sticks and thyme; cook until carrots are heated through. Stir in yogurt cheese and season with salt and pepper to taste. Toss with linguine, sprinkle parsley or chervil and cheese over the top. Serves 4.

Yogurt Cheese
1 pt. plain yogurt

Spoon yogurt into a fine stainless strainer lined with cheesecloth or a paper coffee filter, set over a bowl. For nonfat cheese, use nonfat yogurt. Cover and refrigerate; drain overnight. Discard liquid, transfer yogurt back to the bowl. Stir until smooth and bring to room temperature when ready to use.

Portobello Giblet Dressing

*A dressing any turkey
could be proud to shroud.*

10 to 12-lb. turkey

1/4 cup butter

1 onion, coarsely chopped

Turkey giblets, finely chopped

2 cups chopped mushrooms

4 cups crustless day-old bread
cubes or cornbread crumbs

1/4 cup chopped Italian
parsley

1/2 cup chopped celery

1 teaspoon dried-leaf tarragon

3/4 teaspoon salt

1/8 teaspoon nutmeg

1 cup milk, stock or melted
butter

2 eggs, slightly beaten

1 cup coarsely chopped
walnuts or pecans

Thaw turkey if frozen, rinse thoroughly and refrigerate until ready
to stuff. In a large skillet, melt butter and sauté onion with giblets
until tender. Add mushrooms and sauté 5 minutes more. Mix in
remaining ingredients. Stuff the turkey and roast in a 325F (160C)
oven 35 minutes per pound. Follow directions on turkey package.
Serves 6.

Portobello Soufflé

*Present this soufflé piled high
with portly portobellos.
Excellent use of this
cultivated agaricus.*

4 to 6 large portobello
  mushrooms, to cover
  soufflé

6 tablespoons butter

1 medium onion, chopped

2 tablespoons flour

1 cup chicken stock, page 29

4 beaten egg yolks (or egg
  substitute)

1/2 teaspoon lemon juice

4 egg whites, stiffly beaten

1/2 cup Parmesan cheese

Parsley for garnish

Butter an 8-cup casserole. Preheat oven to 350F (175C). Clean
mushrooms, remove and chop stems, reserving whole caps. Melt
2 tablespoons butter in large skillet, add chopped stems and cook
for 5 minutes over medium heat. Remove from pan and set aside.
Add 2 tablespoons butter to skillet, add onions and sauté until
transparent. Add flour, stirring constantly to make a golden roux.
Add chicken stock and stir until slightly thickened. Add sautéed
mushroom stems and let cool. Stir in beaten egg yolks and lemon
juice. Gently fold in beaten egg whites.

   Place mixture in prepared casserole and bake 40 minutes or
until puffy and brown. Meanwhile, butter a baking sheet, melt
remaining 2 tablespoons butter and brush mushroom caps. Place
caps stem-side down on baking sheet, sprinkle with Parmesan
cheese and bake 350F (175C) 15 minutes. Just before serving,
arrange mushrooms on top of soufflé and garnish with parsley.
Serves 6.

Risotto with Chicken-of-the-Woods Mushrooms

The heart of this creamy risotto is the delicate chicken-of-the-woods mushroom, its yellow-orange color enhanced with golden saffron.

4 tablespoons olive oil

1 small onion, finely chopped

2 cups arborio rice

1/2 cup dry white wine

1 lb. chicken-of-the-woods mushrooms, coarsely chopped

5 cups chicken broth

1 pinch of saffron softened in 1 tablespoon water, if desired

Salt and pepper to taste

2 tablespoons unsalted butter cut in small cubes

1/4 cup grated Parmesan cheese

In a large skillet with a tightly fitting lid, heat oil. Add onion and sauté about 3 minutes until soft. Add rice and stir to coat. Add wine and mushrooms and cook, stirring frequently until liquid is absorbed. Pour in broth and saffron. Add salt and pepper to taste. Reduce heat to low, cover and cook until liquid is absorbed, about 30 minutes. To serve, add butter, stir to melt, and mix in Parmesan cheese. Serves 4.

Green Lentil Curry with Mushrooms
(Dhingri Kari)

A spicy treat from India.

3/4 cup lentils, rinsed

4 cups chicken stock, page 29

2 tablespoons margarine or
  butter

1 onion, finely chopped

1 inch fresh ginger root, peeled
  and finely chopped

1 teaspoon ground cardamom

1 teaspoon garam masala*

1-1/2 teaspoons cumin seed

1/2 teaspoon mustard seed,
  roasted

1 teaspoon coriander seed,
  crushed

1 tablespoon oil

1 lb. button or brown mushrooms, coarsely chopped

1 carrot, diced

1/2 cup water, if needed

2 tablespoons cider vinegar

Salt and pepper to taste

Cilantro and lemon slices for
  garnish

In a large covered Dutch oven place lentils and chicken stock.
Bring to a boil, turn off heat, cover and let stand 1 hour to absorb
stock. In a small saucepan melt margarine and sauté onion, ginger,
spices and seeds for 5 to 8 minutes. Add to lentils and bring to a
boil, cover and reduce heat to simmer. In the same saucepan heat
oil, add mushrooms and fry over high heat for 2 minutes, turning
to cook evenly. Add mushrooms and carrot to simmering lentils.
Add water if more liquid is needed. Cook about 30 minutes, or
until lentils are tender. Add vinegar, salt and pepper. Serve with
cilantro and lemon slices. Serves 4.

* Garam masala is a spice available in Middle Eastern markets.

Mushroom Ratatouille

Many types of mushrooms can be used in this dish, from buttons to a mix of your own choosing. A few dried porcini will soak up the juices to wonderful effect.

4 tablespoons olive oil

1 medium onion, finely chopped

1 garlic clove, finely chopped

14 oz. mixed mushrooms, uniformly sliced

2 large tomatoes, seeded and chopped

1 medium eggplant, cut into 1/2-inch strips

2 celery ribs, finely chopped

6 black olives, pitted

1 teaspoon fresh or dried rosemary

3/4 cup white wine

Salt and pepper to taste

In a large, heavy pan, heat oil and sauté onion over low heat until wilted. Add garlic and sauté until tender. Add mushrooms, tomatoes, eggplant, celery, olives, rosemary, wine, salt and pepper. Cover and cook over low heat for 30 minutes. Vegetables cook in their own juices. To allow vegetables to retain their shape, do not stir. Serves 4.

This is a good dish to cook in your clay pot. Sauté the onions and garlic in a small pan; add ingredients to prepared clay pot, cover and cook as directed.

Rice Djon-Djon

This savory rice dish comes from Bali.

2 cups dried shiitake mushrooms

1-1/2 cups cold water

2 garlic cloves, chopped

2 tablespoons peanut oil

2 teaspoons dried red-pepper flakes

2 whole cloves

4 sprigs cilantro or 1/2 teaspoon cumin powder

1/2 cup thinly sliced onion

3/4 cup raw rice

Soak mushrooms; drain and chop. In a 3-quart saucepan, bring water to a boil and add mushrooms, garlic, peanut oil, red pepper flakes, cloves, cilantro or cumin powder, onion and rice. Cut a round of brown paper, as from a grocery bag, the same circumference as the saucepan. Place paper round over ingredients in pot and cover pot with lid. Turn heat to low and cook for 30 or 35 minutes until rice is tender. Remove paper. Serves 4.

Dried shiitake mushrooms may be labeled as Asian or black Asian mountain mushrooms.

Wild Mushroom and Gruyère Tart

Meaty wild mushrooms, gentle Gruyère, a glass of good wine and a simple salad become the ingredients for a charming luncheon.

1-1/2 cups all-purpose flour

1/4 teaspoon salt

1/2 cup butter, cut in pieces

1 egg yolk

2 or 3 tablespoons water

Mushroom Filling

1 oz. dried mushrooms, soaked and drained or 1 lb. fresh mixed wild mushrooms

1 tablespoon butter

1 shallot, finely chopped

1/4 lb. Gruyère cheese, grated

3 eggs, slightly beaten

1 cup whipping cream

Pepper to taste

1/4 teaspoon nutmeg

Preheat oven to 425F (220C). Into large bowl sift flour and salt. Cut in butter to crumb consistency. Add egg yolk and water, mix to firm but pliable dough. Roll out on lightly floured surface; line an 8-inch tart pan. Prick all over with a fork. Chill 15 minutes. Bake 15 minutes. Remove and reduce heat to 375F (190C).

Coarsely chop mushrooms. In a saucepan, melt butter and sauté shallots 4 to 5 minutes until golden. Add chopped mushrooms; cook 3 minutes until tender. Spread over baked pastry shell. In a medium bowl, mix cheese, eggs and cream. Season with pepper to taste. Pour over mushrooms in pastry shell and sprinkle with nutmeg. Bake 35 minutes until filling is set in center. Serves 4.

Wild Rice
with Owl Mushrooms

*A fine dish to accompany
game birds or venison.*

2 tablespoons unsalted butter

3 strips bacon, chopped

1/2 cup finely chopped onion

1/2 cup fresh owl mushrooms

1/2 cup cooked wild rice

1/2 cup cooked white rice

2 tablespoons chopped
  pistachios

In a heavy medium skillet melt butter over medium-high heat. Add bacon and cook for 4 minutes, turning frequently. Add onion and mushrooms and cook 3 to 4 minutes or until onions begin to brown. Mix with cooked rice. Sprinkle with pistachios. Serves 4.

Owl mushrooms or Hydnum repandum *are so called because they have scales and look like tiny owls sitting on the ground. They are also called* urchins; *others call them* hedgehog *and* lamb foot. *However you see them, they are easily identified by their down-hanging teeth.*

Mushrooms Smetana

Mushrooms give this tasty and familiar dish a new reason for being. Use buttons, chanterelles or Armillaria mellea. Named for Czech composer Bedřich Smetana.

4 tablespoons butter

2 medium onions, thinly sliced

5 stalks celery, finely chopped

1 lb. small button or brown mushrooms

1 tablespoon flour

1 cup hot chicken stock, page 29

Salt and pepper to taste

1 teaspoon mixed fresh herbs such as marjoram, thyme, tarragon and dill

1/3 cup sour cream

Parsley for garnish, finely chopped

Melt butter in a large skillet and sauté onions and celery until transparent. Add mushrooms, turn heat to medium high and cook 2 minutes until mushrooms release their juices. Stir in flour and cook 1 minute, stirring constantly. Add hot stock, salt, pepper and herbs. Simmer over low heat 8 to 10 minutes. Remove from heat and stir in sour cream. Reheat gently, but do not boil.
Sprinkle with parsley. Serves 4.

Sauces

Cèpes Sauce

This sauce is memorable with grilled meats or salmon and as a companion to pasta.

1 oz. dried cèpes

3 cups water for soaking

2 tablespoons butter

2 tablespoons finely chopped onion

1 teaspoon sugar

1 teaspoon salt

1 tablespoon cornstarch

1/4 cup cold water

In a 3-quart saucepan, bring cèpes to boil in 3 cups water. Reduce heat to low and simmer 20 minutes.

While mushrooms are simmering, melt butter in a large skillet and sauté onion with sugar and salt until onions are transparent. Add cèpes and boiling liquid and continue simmering until liquid is reduced by half. Strain through a fine sieve, discard solids. Return sauce to saucepan; dissolve cornstarch in water and stir into pan. Heat, stirring constantly until thickened to desired consistency. Makes 2 cups.

Cèpes are also known as porcini, boletes *and, in Germany,* steinpilz.

Creamy Mushroom Sauce

Believe it! No cream or butter in this sauce though its texture belies the fact. This is so good you'll want to serve it often, over chicken, veal or pork, and over pasta. Hydnum or lamb's foot mushrooms are just right for this dish.

3 tablespoons olive oil

1/4 cup onion, finely chopped

1/4 cup carrot, finely chopped

2 garlic cloves, minced

1/2 teaspoon curry powder

4 cups low-salt chicken broth

1 sprig fresh rosemary or
  1/4 teaspoon dried
  rosemary leaves

2 teaspoons fresh tarragon
  or 1 teaspoon dried-leaf
  tarragon, crushed

1 tablespoon minced shallot

1 teaspoon fresh lemon juice

2 cups chopped fresh
  mushrooms

In a large skillet over medium high heat 1-1/2 tablespoons oil. Add onion, carrot and garlic. Sauté about 8 minutes until vegetables are tender, stirring frequently. Add curry and sauté 2 minutes more. Add broth, rosemary and tarragon and bring to a boil. Reduce heat to medium and cook about 25 minutes until reduced to 1-1/2 cups. Remove from skillet and set aside. In same skillet heat remaining oil. Add shallots and sauté until wilted. Add lemon juice. Increase heat to medium high, add mushrooms and cook about 3 minutes until tender. Combine with vegetables and heat. Makes 2 cups.

Flammulina Sauce with Apples

With the fragrance of sweet and tart apples, this sauce is a culinary coup served over shimmery cellophane noodles.

8 cups water

1 tablespoon salt

6 oz. cellophane noodles

2 tablespoons butter

2 cups flammulina or oyster mushrooms

1 cup finely chopped shallots

1/2 cup julienne strips peeled apple

1 tablespoon Calvados (apple brandy)

Salt and pepper to taste

In a large kettle, bring water to a boil. Add 1 teaspoon salt and noodles; turn off heat. Let noodles stand in their cooking water until ready to serve. In a large skillet, melt butter over high heat; add mushrooms and sauté with shallots and apples for 1 minute. Add Calvados, salt and pepper and cook 1 minute more. Drain noodles and serve with sauce. Serves 4.

Morel Sauce

A sauce that is truly supportive to various dishes. Serve over baguette slices, rice or pasta.

1/2 oz. dried morels

1/4 cup milk

1/4 cup dry white wine

3 tablespoons butter

2 shallots, finely chopped

3 tablespoons flour

1 (12 oz.) can evaporated skim milk

1/4 teaspoon nutmeg

Salt and pepper to taste

1 tablespoon chives, chopped

Soak morels in milk and wine until soft. Drain, reserving liquid, and squeeze dry. In a medium skillet over medium heat melt butter, add shallots and sauté about 4 minutes until light brown. Mix in flour, stirring until smooth and golden. Whisk in milk and bring to a boil. Add soaking liquid, nutmeg, salt and pepper. Bring back to a boil, reduce heat to simmer and cook to desired consistency. Adjust seasoning. Garnish with chives. Makes 1 cup.

Morel, Morchella esculenta, *is a spring mushroom that grows in grassy spots among birches. Excellent eating!*

Porcini Sabayon

Served over grilled meats, rice or pasta, this divine custardy sauce will leave your guests breathless.

1/2 oz. dried porcini, soaked

6 egg yolks or 4 oz. egg substitute

2 teaspoons Worcestershire sauce

2 teaspoons fresh tarragon leaves or 1/2 teaspoon dried-leaf tarragon

1 tablespoon red wine vinegar

1 cup chicken stock for light meats, beef for dark meats, pages, 29 and 31

1 lb. fresh mushrooms

4 tablespoons unsalted butter

Soak mushrooms in water, set aside. Use a double boiler or place a medium mixing bowl over small pan of simmering water. Bottom of bowl must not touch water. Place yolks or egg substitute in top of double boiler or bowl and whisk in Worcestershire, tarragon and vinegar. Slowly whisk in stock, simmering and whisking until mix becomes a frothy consistency. Remove from heat and keep warm. Slice both fresh and soaked mushrooms. Melt butter in a medium skillet over medium-high heat. Add mushrooms and sauté 2 or 3 minutes until tender, stirring often. Carefully fold the sauce into mushrooms. Serve over your favorite meat or vegetable.
Makes 2 cups.

Sabayon *is the French word for custard sauce.*

Purée des Champignons

*Crowning glory for a vegetable dish,
a topping for chops,
roast or fowl, and, of course
a delicious sauce for pasta
or baked potato.*

2 oz. unsalted butter

1 lb. mixed mushrooms, minced

6 tablespoons whipping cream

1 tablespoon flour

1/4 teaspoon nutmeg

1/4 teaspoon salt

In a large skillet over medium-high heat, melt butter; add mushrooms and sauté quickly. In a small saucepan heat the cream, but do not let it boil. When mushrooms have released their liquids and the moisture has cooked away, add the hot cream, mix in flour and stir constantly until smooth and creamy. Place in food processor or blender with nutmeg and salt and process to smooth consistency. Makes 2 cups.

Steak Sauce with Honey Mushrooms

A robust sauce that gives steak a savory, stylish new flavor. If available use Armillaria mellea or honey mushrooms.

4 tablespoons butter

1/2 cup finely chopped shallots

1/2 lb. mushrooms

1-1/2 cups dry red wine

1 bay leaf

1/4 teaspoon dried thyme leaves

1 tablespoon parsley, chopped

2 teaspoons Bovril® sauce or meat extract*

1/4 cup butter

1 tablespoon lemon juice

1 teaspoon flour

Salt and pepper to taste

4 sprigs parsley for garnish

In a large saucepan melt 4 tablespoons butter over medium heat. Add shallots and mushrooms; cook about 5 minutes until soft. Pour in wine, add bay leaf, thyme and parsley; cook until liquid is reduced to 3/4 cup. Remove bay leaf and discard. Stir in Bovril® sauce; set pan aside. In a small bowl cream 1/4 cup butter. Beat vigorously into mushroom mixture along with lemon juice and flour. Scrape loose bits from pan. Add salt and pepper to taste. Keep hot until serving. Garnish with parsley sprigs. Makes 1 cup.

* Bovril® sauce may be found in specialty markets with meat extract and bouillon products.

Wood Ear Sauce

Wood ear mushrooms give an irresistible taste to this sauce for omelet, rice, meats or pasta. Remember, wood ear swells voluminously as it soaks, so give it room.

1/2 oz. dried wood ear mushrooms

3 cups chicken, veal or beef broth

2 teaspoons oyster sauce

2 teaspoons hoisin sauce

1/2 teaspoons five-spice powder

1 garlic clove, minced

1-1/2 tablespoons cornstarch

1/4 cup cold water

In a large bowl, soak mushrooms in 2 cups water. In 3-quart covered saucepan heat broth over medium-high heat. Add soaked, drained wood ear and bring to a boil. Reduce heat and simmer, covered, for 1 hour. Remove mushrooms from stock with slotted spoon, cut into small pieces, return to liquid. Add oyster sauce, hoisin sauce, five-spice powder and garlic. Bring back to a simmer. Dissolve cornstarch in water, stir into mushroom sauce, stirring constantly until smooth and creamy. Makes 1 cup.

You can find wood ear, both dried and fresh, oyster sauce, hoisin sauce and five-spice powder in Asian food sections or specialty markets.

Tales from the Hunt

Along with a husky Siberian, a Siberian Husky, and a dozen guides who had pieced together an exquisitely complicated network of contacts in this little-traveled corner of the world, our group of 15 was airlifted by helicopter from a deserted meadow in eastern Russia near the Manchurian border, to the hills of Kamchatka. We were there to hunt Borivicki, the Russian boletes, but the clouds opened and we were rainstuck for two days. Our network turned up a regional shaman, Tatjana of the Koryak people, a childlike, beautiful-countenanced, energetic 72-year-old ball of fire who thrilled us as she whirled, chanted and beat her drum, calling upon the spirits to bring forth fruits for our picking. Which they did . . . in abundance, both mushrooms *and* blueberries. She stayed with us in our camp, our interpreters conveying Tatjana's delight in our appreciation of the Borivicki, which led her to dance again and again, changing costume as she evoked the moves of raven, bear and deer . . . beautifully beaded fur-lined suede dress and beaded braids, then a snow-white suit with fur hood. She sang, twanging a bow and punctuating her legends with heartfelt beats of deerskin drum . . . all stretched and strung, beaded and sewn by her own hand. We spoke through interpreters, but communicated without words. When time came to prepare mushrooms, we instantly had stove-top rapport.

Miscellaneous

Mushroom Candy!

A healthy treat that's not too sweet.

1 lb. button mushrooms, chopped

1 cup apple juice

1 teaspoon anise flavoring

2 tablespoons gelatin

1/2 cup apple or orange juice

Sugar to taste

Turbinado (raw sugar) for coating

Boil mushrooms in apple juice until juice has almost evaporated. Add anise flavoring. Dissolve gelatin in apple or orange juice. Add to mushroom-fruit-juice mixture; add sugar to taste. Let cool. Form into shapes and roll in turbinado to coat. Makes 20.

In Russia hordes of Muscovites board the Metro at 4 in the morning. Their laps are loaded with mushroom baskets. They scramble to be the first in the woods to collect mushrooms to feed their families.

Clavaria Crisp

This is a sweet mushroom and this recipe is for dessert. The only substiute for clavaria would be the common button, but it would not be nearly as delicious.

Topping, below

1 tablespoon butter

1/2 lb. clavaria mushrooms, coarsely chopped

1 ripe persimmon, peeled, mashed

1 tablespoon lemon juice

1 teaspoon ground cinnamon

1/4 teaspoon ground ginger

Butter a shallow 8-inch-square baking dish. Preheat oven to 375F (190C). Melt butter in a skillet over medium-high heat, add chopped mushrooms and cook 3 minutes until tender. Combine with persimmon, lemon juice, cinnamon and ginger. Put into prepared baking dish and crumble topping over the top. Bake 30 minutes or until crust is golden brown. Serves 4.

Topping
3/4 cup flour

4 tablespoons powdered sugar

4 tablespoons unsalted butter

Mix flour, sugar and butter and cut together with a fork or 2 knives until of crumb consistency.

Clavariaceae—when you come upon these, they look like undersea coral formations, both in conformation and color. They are exquisite, and also make a good addition to a salad.

India's Samosas

Northern India is where I first encountered these delicious bites. That time they were made with deer mushrooms, Latin name Pluteus cervinus. *These mini pies are excellent snacks or hors d'oeuvres.*

Pastry, next page, or
  12 wonton wrappers

3 potatoes, peeled, cooked

4 tablespoons oil

2 onions, finely chopped

1 garlic clove, minced

1/2 teaspoon cumin

1/2 teaspoon ground
  coriander

1/2 teaspoon garam masala*

1/4 teaspoon turmeric

1 cup chopped okra

1 cup chopped fresh spinach

4 carrots, peeled and grated

6 choice mushrooms,
  chopped, stems removed

2 teaspoons lemon juice

4 tablespoons vegetable oil

Oil for frying

---

* Garam masala is a spice mix available in Middle Eastern stores. It is great to have handy in your vocabulary of spices to lend its piquancy to many ethnic dishes.

Chop cooked potatoes. In a large skillet heat 4 tablespoons oil. Add onions, garlic, cumin, coriander, garam masala and turmeric. Cook, stirring constantly, 5 minutes. Add potatoes, okra, spinach, carrots and mushrooms. Cook 5 minutes more. Add lemon juice. Place a spoonful of mixture in the center of each pastry square and, with dampened fingers, press edges together. In a wok heat vegetable oil to sizzling then reduce to medium heat. Fry a few at a time about 3 minutes until golden brown. Makes 12 samosas.

Pastry
1/2 cup whole-wheat flour
1/2 cup vegetable oil
1/2 teaspoon salt
1/2 cup water

In a bowl, mix together flour, oil, salt and water. Stir and knead until smooth. On a lightly floured surface, roll out dough with a rolling pin to 9 x 12 inches. Cut into 12 3-inch squares.

Fluted Mushroom Sauté

An attractive way to enhance store-bought button mushrooms is to cut them into whirligigs and sauté them. Use as a side dish or a quick hors d'oeuvre.

1/4 lb. mushroom caps
1 tablespoon butter
Salt and pepper to taste
Lemon wedge

To flute mushrooms: Wipe with paper towels. Cut off stems so that they are even with caps. With a small curved knife or lemon zester, beginning at the center, cut grooves that spiral to the edges of the mushroom cap.

To sauté: In a large skillet over medium-high heat, melt the butter. When hot and foaming, add the mushrooms, salt and pepper and a squeeze of lemon juice. Toss and sauté for 3 minutes.

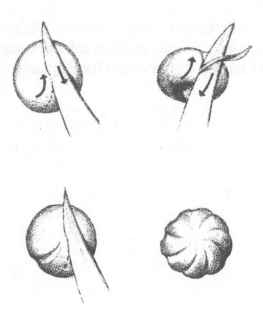

Mushroom Dumplings

Delectable morsels to accompany a stew or to add to a broth or soup.

6 slices white bread, soaked in water to cover

1 teaspoon grated onion

2 egg yolks

12 medium mushrooms or 6 oz. wild mix, finely chopped

2 tablespoons minced parsley

3 tablespoons dry bread-crumbs

Salt and pepper to taste

3 egg whites, stiffly beaten

Butter a 9-inch pie pan. Preheat oven to 375F (190C). Soak bread in water, then press or squeeze out all moisture. Place bread in a medium bowl and stir in onion to make a smooth paste. Add egg yolks, mushrooms, parsley and enough breadcrumbs to make a thick paste. Season with salt and pepper and fold in beaten egg whites. Spread mixture in prepared pie pan and bake for 20 minutes or until lightly browned. Mold into balls with two small spoons or scoop out with melon baller and serve in hot soup. Makes 10 balls.

Mushroom Duxelles

You will never be without this treasure once you've tasted it. Store duxelles in the freezer for a fabulous appetizer spread or to add to soups, top pasta, stuff pork, lamb or fowl, layer in a casserole, or create something new of your own.

3 tablespoons butter

2/3 cup finely minced onion

1 cup dried mushrooms, soaked and drained or 2 cups fresh mushrooms, finely minced

1/4 teaspoon salt

1/4 teaspoon sugar

1/2 teaspoon soy sauce

In a medium skillet over medium-high heat, melt butter and sauté onion until transparent. Add mushrooms, salt, sugar and soy sauce, stirring constantly. Cook until liquid evaporates and mixture becomes paste-like. Cool for 1/2 hour. Place in covered container and refrigerate or freeze until needed. Makes 1 cup.

Variation: For basil duxelles, add 2 tablespoons fresh chopped basil to basic recipe, or add any herbs you choose.

Mushroom Fritters

Really good party food, best with yellow foot, oyster, Hydnum repandum or agaricus.

1-1/2 cups all-purpose flour

1 teaspoon salt

1/4 teaspoon pepper

1 tablespoon melted butter or oil

2 beaten egg yolks

3/4 cup flat beer

2 egg whites, stiffly beaten

6 cups cooking oil

25 fresh mushrooms

2 tablespoons parsley, minced

Lemon wedges

Preheat oven to 300F (150C). In a large bowl mix flour, salt, pepper, butter and egg yolks. Gradually add beer. Stir, cover and allow to rest in the refrigerator for 3 to 12 hours. Just before using, fold in beaten egg whites. In a large kettle or fryer heat the oil to 350F (180C). Dip the mushrooms in the batter and with a slotted spoon put in the hot oil to fry. Fry 3 or 4 minutes or until golden. Make sure the mushrooms are dry when you dip them so that batter will adhere. Don't crowd the mushrooms while they are frying; do them in small batches. Drain on paper towels. Keep warm on baking sheet in oven. Sprinkle with parsley and serve with lemon wedges. Makes 25 fritters.

Mushroom Powder

*Mushroom powder becomes a
condiment you will reach for
over and over again.
A few shakes will infuse a
soup or stew, and enhance
a gravy or sauce with the
unique flavor of mushroom.*

1/4 lb. dried mushrooms

Grind mushrooms to a powder in blender or electric coffee grinder.
Store in a tightly covered jar away from light. Makes 1/4 cup
powder.

NOTE: Do not use the food processor, because mushrooms will stick
to the blades and will not reduce to powder successfully.

Pickled Honey Mushrooms

Great to have in the pantry for impromptu gifts and condiments for the table.

5 cups water

2-1/2 cups cider vinegar

1/2 cup pickling salt

6 red, green or black peppercorns

1 hot pepper, such as jalapeño or serrano

1 teaspoon dried coriander leaves

1 garlic clove

1 teaspoon fresh basil leaves

1 bay leaf, crumbled

1 teaspoon oregano

1 lb. honey mushrooms

Sterilize 4 pint jars and set aside. In a 10-qt. pan bring water, vinegar, pickling salt, peppercorns, hot pepper, coriander, garlic, basil leaves, bay leaf and oregano to a boil. Clean mushrooms and drop into the boiling mixture. Blanch for 2 minutes. With a ladle, fill prepared jars with mushrooms and liquid to within 1/2 inch of tops. Seal. Place jars in a pan large enough to cover the jars with 2 inches of water. Cover and bring water bath to a boil and boil sealed jars 20 minutes to preserve. At higher altitudes boil 10 minutes longer. Remove from water bath and allow to cool. Makes 4 pints. Keeps indefinitely.

Porcini Oil

Nice to have on hand for sudden attacks of culinary inspiration when you crave a touch of mushroom flavor. Wonderful for salads, or as a gift for someone who loves to cook.

1 oz. dried porcini mushrooms

1/2 cup Burgundy

2 cups extra virgin olive oil or other oil of your choice

Soak the mushrooms in Burgundy for 1/2 hour or more. In a small saucepan boil the mushrooms in their soaking liquid about 5 minutes or until liquid is reduced to 2 teaspoons. Strain off juices, pressing out the liquid for the most intense flavor. Add juices to olive oil and drop in the drained mushrooms. When you have used the oil, replenish your supply with more oil over the mushrooms. Makes 2-1/2 cups.

Scrambled Eggs and Chanterelles

*Celebrate breakfast
or serve as post-theater treat.*

1/4 lb. fresh chanterelles or
    other mushrooms

6 eggs, room temperature

2 tablespoons butter

2 tablespoons cream

Salt and pepper to taste

2 tablespoons fresh chopped
    chives

In a medium saucepan bring water to a boil, drop in fresh mushrooms and blanch for 1 minute. Remove from water and drain on paper towel, chop coarsely. In a small bowl beat eggs with whisk until blended, not frothy. In a medium skillet over medium heat melt butter, cook the eggs stirring constantly until eggs begin to set. Add cream and mushrooms, stir and cook to desired degree of doneness. Season with salt and pepper and garnish with chives. Serves 4.

Mushroom Extract

This sumptuous extract enriches any recipe to which you may add it— an omelet, a sauce for meat or game, a touch to a vegetable creation—dramatically altering flavor and aroma

1 oz. dried wild mushrooms

3 cups water, wine, milk, stock, vodka, coffee, tea or liquid of your choice.

In a small saucepan over medium-high heat, bring mushrooms and liquid to a boil. Reduce heat to low and simmer until reduced to 1 cup. Place in food processor and blend. Refrigerate, covered, until needed.

The best extracts are made from boletes and morels. Freeze in ice-cube trays and transfer to a freezer bag to ensure you will always have a quick infusion of mushroom flavor on hand.

Index